Leadership under Construction

Creating Paths toward Transformation

H. Darrell Young
Joseph P. Hester

ScarecrowEducation
Lanham, Maryland • Toronto • Oxford
2004

Published in the United States of America
by ScarecrowEducation
An imprint of The Rowman & Littlefield Publishing Group, Inc.
4501 Forbes Boulevard, Suite 200, Lanham, Maryland 20706
www.scaroweducation.com

PO Box 317
Oxford
OX2 9RU, UK

British Library Cataloguing in Publication Information Available

Library of Congress Cataloging-in-Publication Data

Young, H. Darrell, 1948–
  Leadership under construction : creating paths toward transformation.
/ H. Darrell Young, Joseph P. Hester.
      p. cm.
Includes bibliographical references.
  ISBN 1-57886-106-3 (pbk. : alk. paper)
  1. Leadership. I. Hester, Joseph P. II. Title.
  HD57.7 .Y684 2004
  658.4'092—dc22

                                          2003023441

♾™ The paper used in this publication meets the minimum requirements of American National
Standard for Information Sciences—Permanence of Paper for Printed Library Materials,
ANSI/NISO Z39.48-1992. Manufactured in the United States of America.

This book is dedicated to our wives, students, and former business associates without whom our leadership capacity would be greatly diminished.

Contents

Acknowledgments

My attention was drawn to the study of leadership during the mid-1980s. I had become president of a major computer software company specializing in developing software for the healthcare industry. As a result of my new responsibilities and the acceleration of environmental change in our industry, I began a renewed leadership self-development journey. As I began my journey, I chose Warren Bennis as my guide. Dr. Bennis has observed, researched, and lived leadership for more than four decades, which has resulted in over twenty five books on the subject. He has been highly influential in my own development as a business leader and stimulated my personal study of leadership.

During the past fifteen years, I have also had the opportunity to read and study hundreds of books and articles authored by leading leadership professionals. This study has gradually formed my own leadership philosophy and style and has provided the foundation for the development of this leadership-training manual.

Although it is impossible to mention every author whose work has influenced the development of this manual, a thorough bibliography has been included that mentions many of these works. In this space I would like to mention some of those authors whose ideas have provided the foundation of my own leadership philosophy. Among these are Michael H. Annison, Bruce Barton, Warren Bennis, Kenneth Blanchard, Kevin Cashman, Max DePree, Peter F. Drucker, Ted Engstrom, Leighton Ford, Mark A. Frohman, Robert Greenleaf, Craig R. Hickman, John R. Kotter, James M. Kouzes, Robert C. Larson, John C. Maxwell, Calvin Miller, Burt Nanus, Perry Pascarella, Donald T. Philips, Berry Z. Posner, Andrew Stanley, and Margaret J. Weatley.

Finally, I would also like to acknowledge the work of Dr. Joseph P. Hester, who was able to take my notes, bring style and organization to my writing, provide transitions and shore up areas needing additional information, and developed many of the activities for this manual.

H. Darrell Young

LEADERSHIP CONCEPTS FOR BUILDING A LEADERSHIP CULTURE

Leadership under Construction is a workbook of leadership concepts that provides individuals and organizations a leadership development tool that is reflective of the times in which we live. Too often our leadership journey begins as a matter of default, or as a result of being chosen, rather than as a decision of personal choice. As a result, we often attend seminars on leadership or read books and/or book reviews on the practical *how to's* of leadership. Unfortunately, the *how to's* provide little understanding of the *concepts* and *principles* of leadership and their connections and interconnections with each other. Therefore, our attention is merely directed to the situation at hand, rather than to developing long-lasting leadership *concepts* and *principles*.

Every construction project requires both contractors (concepts) and sub-contractors (applications). The issue is one of priority. Becoming an ethical and effective leader is not easy. In fact, becoming a leader is hard work; work that requires patience and persistence. It can also be complex due the fact that leadership requires knowledge of principles and concepts, and means for building human relationships and resolving the conflicts among people that naturally occur.

All of us have been chosen to become leaders, the only question is whether or not we will accept the challenge and make the choice to learn to lead. It is becoming increasingly difficult to lead because of the accelerating and pervasive forces of change. These forces include the complexities of the environment, the legal as well as the ethical parameters of our work, the difficulties of growing our work from our inner characters. Even the culture of relativism works against maintaining personal and work-centered standards in the face of a multinational and multicultural workforce. All of these issues and conditions are interconnected and it is the leader who must deal with them in a forthright manner. The uncertainty and unpredictability that results from these new challenges reinforce the increased need for self-development. Our leadership behaviors, persistence, and consistency are acquired through lifelong learning, efficient problem solving, and choosing an inner path of ethical living.

IT IS THE DESIRE OF THE AUTHORS OF THIS WORKBOOK THAT IT BECOMES A SELF-DEVELOPMENT TOOL THAT SUPPORTS STUDENTS AND TEACHERS IN BUILDING A CONCEPTUAL FOUNDATION FOR LEADERSHIP.

In the pages below are three global concepts that categorize the definition of "leadership." Within the framework of these concepts you will learn about the essential characteristics of leadership, how these concepts are interconnected, and begin building a foundation for your own leadership development. These concepts are the following:

STRATEGIC THINKING

Unity without Uniformity

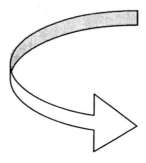 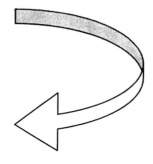

CONTINUOUS IMPROVEMENT

Transformation Not Promises

BUILDING RELATIONSHIPS

Leaders Growing Leaders

The Three-Legged Stool

We can best picture leadership as a *three-legged stool*. Leadership is the seat of the stool that can move in any direction—as circumstances and need demands. The three legs of the stool that support the seat of leadership are the three fundamental concepts illustrated above: Strategic Thinking, Continuous Improvement, and Building Relationships. The rungs holding these three supports together and thus completing the foundation of leadership are our *values, beliefs,* and *purposes.* This is a rich metaphor for illustrating the requirements and foundations of leadership. Based on the events of the last five years, there seems to be a shortage of leaders in the 21st century who understand this concept. Furthermore, many do not understand that there are new problems, new opportunities, and a new world to be won. We can conclude that it is time for a new generation of leadership and a new kind of leader.

However, it has become increasingly difficult to confine the concept of leadership to a few words or phrases—witness the hundreds of books that have been written about leadership during the past twenty years. As a result, there are more than 500 definitions of "leadership" in use today (Bennis, HBO & Company Conference, 1990). So we see that it is easy to understand how there would be disagreement and misunderstanding about what a leader is and does, and exactly how a person becomes a leader.

Leadership, we will discover, is an endless process of learning and relearning what study and experience teaches us. It is not a destination, but a lifelong journey of self-appraisal. We really can't teach it to you; leadership must be learned and earned. Therefore, leaders *choose to become leaders.* Jim Whittaker, the first American to climb Mt. Everest, said, "You never conquer the mountain, you conquer yourself, your doubts and your fears." Likewise, pertaining to leadership, we never conquer it; we can, however, conquer our doubts and fears about becoming a leader.

Those who have conquered their doubts and fears about becoming leaders have looked beyond their self-interest and focused on what needs to be done, not what they personally desire. Leaders are concerned—not with their persona—but with getting the job done, making a difference, and growing other leaders. Because their purpose is to serve those whom they lead, they tolerate diversity and creativity, but are intolerant when it comes to a person's performance, standards, and values. Leaders are responsible to the mission of their organizations and hold themselves accountable, as well as those whom they lead.

These same leaders are not afraid of the strengths of their associates. They, in fact, get excited about them. The servant-leader is confident, and has a consuming sincerity and an overwhelming belief in the importance of the work to be done. They readily submit themselves to self-evaluation as an act of re-creation—to make sure they are the person they are striving to become. They understand that the foundation of leadership is character and that character reflects who and what we actually are, not what others think we are.

As educators (and students), if we intend to develop a new generation of leaders, we need to study and understand the requirements of 21st-century leadership. We must also come to grips with two vastly different paradigms: the *self-directed* leader versus the *other-directed* leader. These paradigms have created a paradox for leadership that demands further analysis and clarification. A major purpose of this workbook and the two that follow is to examine these differences and focus on the qualities of the ethical and servant leader.

This workbook is called *Leadership under Construction* because you are just beginning to focus on leadership principles and concepts and build yourself the disposition of a leader. It is created for both students and teachers to use together. The teacher or facilitator who brings you this material is looked upon as a general contractor, a catalyst of thought, knowledge, and understanding. The teacher will assist students apply the principles and concepts of leadership and bring continuous attention to how they are interconnected.

Workbook exercises for students have been developed and used liberally throughout this training guide to facilitate student learning and real-life applications of leadership principles. These exercises can be used in a variety of ways and the teacher-facilitator of this material should make an effort to find a comfort zone for his or her abilities and capacities. They can be reorganized for use with individuals, small groups, or larger classes and organizations. It is important not to forget the individual student when teaching. After all, each person is required to learn and apply these concepts for him or herself.

FEEDBACK

Before we proceed, the students need to reconsider the personal value of pursuing a study of self-development beyond attending these classes at the request of a sponsor. One way of generating dialogue about this commitment is to ask them the following questions:

1. What's in it for me?
2. Why should I commit myself to learning the concepts of leadership?

It is always sound to ask for the student's perspective before giving too many answers. Giving too much too quickly often shuts down students' thinking and negates any creative response or question they might have. In the box below are some of the answers I've learned *play* well with students. Experience has taught that these answers should be presented in a way that is consistent with the content of the student workbook:

LEADERSHIP TRAINING TEACHES THE FOLLOWING:

FIRST:

- How to define yourself—the person you want to become.
- How to create a future of your own choosing.
- How to use your thinking ability and experience to develop and apply ethical principles to your present and future behaviors.
- The power of a strong, yet flexible foundation.

SECOND:

- How to let go of behaviors that have been responsible for past successes that may cause you to fail in the future.
- How to become a person committed to continuous value improvement.
- The connections between personal transformation and performance.
- How to free yourself from personal biases and adopt a more universal and ethical point of view.

THIRD:

- Ideas, methods, and behaviors for winning friends and influencing people.
- The importance of relationships.
- The necessity of developing and maintaining interconnections.
- The importance of divesting of personal power and investing in the value of others.
- The value of servant leadership.

 *Teaching pointers in italics*

There are five basic "knowns" of leadership. They are the following:

1. Leadership development is a commitment to self-development and is achieved through lifelong learning, thinking, and consistent ethical living.
   (*Leadership development is hard work; it requires following other leaders and embracing unnatural behaviors and disciplines.*)

2. There is no one way to lead.
   (*The student may ask, "What if I'm not capable?" Share with them the lives of George Washington, the warrior, and Thomas Paine, the writer. Ask: "Who had a greater influence on your freedom?"*)

3. Character is the foundation of leadership.
   (*The issue is the quality of your life and the relationships that you build and sustain over a lifetime.*)

4. The cost of leadership is beyond what most people are willing to pay.
   (*No pain, no gain.*)

5. Because nothing happens until someone steps up, everything rises and falls on leadership.
   (*Becoming a leader is your choice.*)

These basic-five are important to your students for the following reasons:

1. Because of the diverse interruptions of leadership, some in your class will believe they cannot lead;

2. Others won't see the value of leading;

3. Some won't understand that leadership is not about power, position, or control—that it's about influence;

4. A few will believe they have already arrived; and

5. Some won't really care.

The teacher's role is to convince students that everyone is capable of leading and everyone should aspire to lead. This is a matter of confidence and understanding.

Ethical Leadership for Public School Administrators and Teachers

A new book written by Dr. Joseph P. Hester and published by McFarland & Company, Inc., focuses on "leading from the inside out," from one's character. The first two chapters of *Ethical Leadership* address this issue:

▶ **"Leadership Need"** focuses on the requirements of leadership and the culture for building leaders.

- The Need for Ethical Leadership
- Building a Leadership Culture
- Leadership Roles

▶ **"Leadership Principles"** focuses on the foundational concepts and principles of leadership, including becoming an ethical and servant leader.

- Leadership Foundations
- Leadership Principles
- Ethical/Servant Leadership

This book can be used as a self-contained workbook. Each chapter has exercises that engage the minds of participants. Here, we are using some of these exercises in conjunction with *Leadership under Construction*. This will give added depth and meaning to this course of study.

Before engaging students in the activities of this workbook, the instructor/facilitator should require that all students read chapters 1 and 2 from *Ethical Leadership*. Students are to complete activities 5, 6, 7, and 8 in chapter 1 and activities 1, 2, and 5 in chapter 2 before moving on to the activities in this student workbook.

PART 1
STRATEGIC THINKING

Unity without Uniformity

Unity without Uniformity is about being of one mind united in what we do and aspiring to make a significant difference in a world of increasing diversity and change. This is never an easy transition for it requires self-evaluation as well as seeking "common goals" within the organization. We need to work from the bottom up—self-definition first, then the organization—however, in the end, the reason we define ourselves is to achieve greater unity with others.

PART 1 EMPHASIZES THREE FUNDAMENTAL CONCEPTS:

Leadership Role Models and Definition

The Foundation of Leadership

Unity of Vision

Unity Without Uniformity

Linking Thought with Purpose

ICE-BREAKERS

One method of breaking down barriers and warming the class to discussion and dialogue is to have them respond to significant quotes. Use your judgment about when and where to use these quotes, but do use them for they bring significant attention to the principles and concepts of leadership.

> *If you don't know who you are, you can't know where you're going.*—Alexander Solzhenitsyn

> *If you don't know where you are going any road will take you there.*—from the *Wizard of Oz*

> *Leadership is an art, a performing art, and in the art of leadership, the artist instrument is "SELF." The mastery of the art of leadership comes with the mastery of self.*—Max Dupree

Leadership Role Models and Definitions

CONCEPT 1.1
Understanding and defining "leadership" is prerequisite to becoming a great leader.

Purpose:

The purpose of this section is to gain agreement and unity as a group on the definition of leadership using historic and known leaders.

Procedures:

- At the beginning of this section, the teacher should introduce the concepts of *strategic thinking* (unity without uniformity), *continuous improvement* (transformance not promises), and *leaders growing leaders* (building relationships, building a leadership culture, or influencing others). These are the basic concepts around which this leadership program is constructed.

  - Activity 3 will further engage students in developing these concepts. Building your teaching around these concepts will give students an organized method of learning and remembering the keys to effective leadership. Activity 3 will enrich their understanding by providing an opportunity for students to create their own definition of "leadership" as a foundation for dialogue with their classmates.

  - Because of the complexity of these concepts, they are introduced by telling four stories: the *earthquake story* is about building foundations for strategic thinking; the *orchestra* story is about the importance of organization; the *monkey story* is about letting go of ineffective methods and engaging in continuous improvement; and the *cable car story* is about influencing others by "running alongside of them" before engaging them in ideas and practices that will change how they operate. "Running alongside of" is an enriching and interesting metaphor for "getting to know others," "understanding them," and "observing their work"

3

before being actually hooked up with them in a dialogue of change and improvement.

- Discuss concept 1.1 with the class. Through discussion, explore its meaning.

- Ask students to nominate particular persons as great leaders. List these on the board. Student choices will include political, religious, civil, and military leaders. Explore with students why each nominee achieved success.

- Ask students to choose leaders they have known personally. List them on the board and discuss the reasons they have chosen these individuals. These will probably include parents, teachers, ministers, coaches, grandparents, peers, and work associates, etc.

- Ask each student to choose one individual from either group. This person will be their subject for completing activities 1 and 2.

- Bring this discussion to a conclusion by completing activity 3, and follow with a discussion of "There Is No One Way to Lead." You may want to put this on an overhead.

- Complete activities 4 and 5. Bring these activities to a conclusion with a discussion of "What Leadership Is Not."

Remember:

It's important that students develop a definition of leadership by presenting the results of their work in activities 1 and 2 to the class for discussion and clarification. Students can present either the historic or personal exercise to the class with the teacher helping them redefine their input through dialogue and discussion. The teacher should guide this discussion to help ensure consistency with the material that follows: "There Is No One Way to Lead: Defining 'Leadership'."

Examples:

- Washington was honest. What you mean is that he was a person of character.

- Washington was determined. What you mean is that he had a value system.

- Washington loved his family. You mean he had beliefs that gave him purpose and foundation.

- Washington tried new things. You mean he was a risk taker; an innovator; and that he embraced change.

Getting these points across to students will not always be easy. You may wish to provide examples other than these and from personal experience or ask students if they can provide additional examples. This helps the entire class to "get at" the concepts being discussed.

Activities:

- The six activities in this section are designed to help students define the concept of "leadership" and become familiar with the characteristics, values, and behaviors of effective leaders.

- Make sure each participant has copies of these activities. You can use them as overheads or handouts. Be sure to clarify any misunderstandings before proceeding.

- The teacher should become familiar with these activities before using them with students. Remember that students learn best when actively engaged and are able to contribute to the class discussion.

Allotted Time:

- The study of leadership works best with at least two, one-hour classes per week over a complete semester of sixteen weeks. This means the teacher will have thirty-two classes to complete the introductory materials and thirteen activities.

- Suggested teaching plan:

  ▶ Week 1: Use "Background" for introduction and include chapters 1 and 2 of *Ethical Leadership*. Build introductory material around the first two class periods. If the class meets three times per week, this will provide even more time for discussion.

  ▶ Weeks 2–7: Activities 1–6 with discussions. For a two-hour class, this provides twelve class periods for these six activities and discussions—plan accordingly.

  ▶ Weeks 8–13: Discussions and activities 7–10. For a two-hour class, this provides twelve class periods for these four activities and discussions.

  ▶ Weeks 14–16: Discussions and activities 11–14. For a two-hour class, this provides six class periods to complete these four activities and wrap up part 1 of this study.

TO THE TEACHER

Before engaging students in activity 1, explain to them that there are many different types of leaders, all with their own style, beliefs, and values. Some may be judged good, others not so good, and still others as just plain bad or morally evil. Some leaders may be morally good at heart and still be ineffective. Examples need to be given and solicited from the class. Sometimes it is effective to look at extremes such as Adolph Hitler. Students are familiar with Hitler and can discuss his methods fairly easily. Students should understand that in any organization, there should be agreement among its members on a style of leadership they believe best represents a leader worth following.

Here are several points of discussion to get you started:

- The Hero—The personification of the organization and the primary source of success.

- The Father Figure—The group wants to be told what to do. This could be an accountability or responsibility issue.

- The Tyrant—The tyrant controls, dominates, and even terrorizes those who follow.

- The Organizer—This leader organizes for cooperative effort.

- The Servant—The servant serves the needs of the organization and its people.

- The Liberator—Seeks to free us from the past and move us into continuous improvement.

- The Ethical Leader—The ethical leader could be a hero, a father figure, an organizer, a servant, or a liberator, but will always treat people with dignity and preserve his or her own moral integrity. Trust, honesty, and fair play are the hallmarks of the ethical leader.

Activity 1: Discussion Matrix for Discovering Why Many Great Historic Leaders Achieved Greatness

Directions: In the middle circle put the name of a great leader that has been listed on the board. In the outer circle, list as many characteristics of this leader as you are able. In the outer box, state the reasons for this leader's greatness.

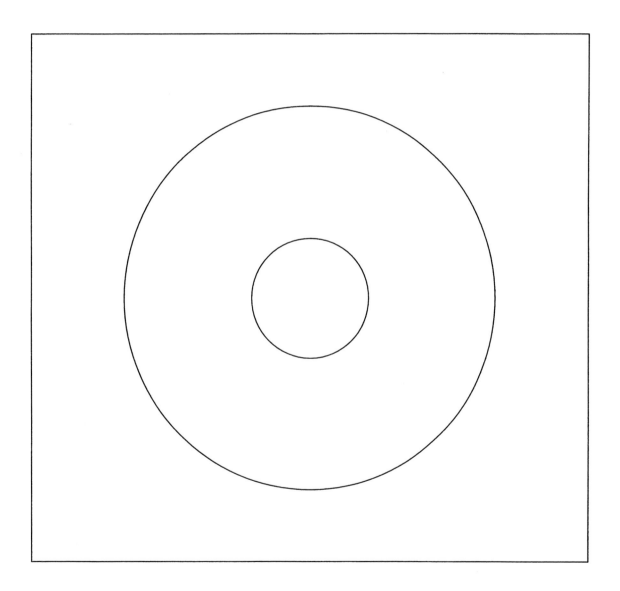

Activity 2: Qualities of Leaders You Have Known Personally

Directions: Choose a leader you have known personally and complete the following activity.

Name of person:_____

Brief narrative describing the person's achievements:

_____

_____

_____

_____

_____

List leadership traits of this person and give examples of each:

_____

_____

_____

_____

_____

_____

Give reasons why you think this person is a great leader:

_____

_____

_____

_____

_____

_____

Activity 3: Classroom Presentation

Directions: Students will consolidate both historic and personally known leadership characteristics (qualities, values, and behaviors) into the following three categories:

1. Strategic Thinking
2. Continuous Improvement
3. Influencing Others

THE CHART ON THE NEXT PAGE—"THERE IS NO ONE WAY TO LEAD"—PROVIDES INFORMATION FOR DEFINING EACH OF THESE TERMS.

As each student presents his/her reasons, the teacher will consolidate the findings on a wall board or wall chart under the headings below:

STRATEGIC THINKING (Unity without uniformity)

_____

_____

_____

_____

CONTINUOUS IMPROVEMENT (Transformance not promises)

_____

_____

_____

_____

INFLUENCING OTHERS (Building a leadership culture)

_____

_____

_____

_____

THERE IS NO ONE WAY TO LEAD
DEFINING "LEADERSHIP"

Foundation

Managing the Environment

"If you don't know where you are going, any road will take you there."

- Determine values and beliefs
- Establish purpose
- Define mission
- Gather facts and determine reality
- Create and communicate a vision of the future
- Develop strategies
- Determine measurements
- Continually reevaluate value
- Maintain an accurate self-assessment
- Storytelling

Continuous Improvement

Managing Self

Leadership is a process of lifelong self-development and change.

- Embrace change as the rule, not the exception
- Identify the external and internal interconnected forces of change
- Balance behaviors and disciplines
- Let go, take risks, and innovate
- Commit oneself to life-long learning and thinking
- Accept adversity as the purification process of leading
- Ensure an ongoing learning environment
- Believe people can change
- Seek counsel

Influencing Others

Serving Others

Leadership inspires trust, creates meaning, and cares for others.

- Attract, recruit, and retain a leadership foundation
- Succession is the measurement of effectiveness
- Develop leadership environments
- Acknowledge new leader's roles as a designer, teacher, and steward
- Divest of yourself and invest in others
- Empower, enable, and serve
- Love the organization, people, and what they do
- Create value through performance, not promises
- Leaders are followers
- Leaders are coaches

In summary, by examining the foundations of leadership and understanding that leadership entails continuous improvement and influencing others, we are able to conclude that leaders are individually gifted and corporately commissioned.

Activity 4: Leadership Characteristics

Directions: Review your definition of "leadership." From your definition, list in order your strongest and weakest leadership characteristics. In the spaces that follow, give reasons for your choices:

Strongest:	Reason:
1.	
2.	
3.	
4.	
5.	

Weakest:	Reason:
1.	
2.	
3.	
4.	
5.	

WHAT LEADERSHIP IS NOT

since we have defined what leadership is.

An executive friend was asked by his fourteen-year-old son to give him a simple bottom-line definition of leadership for a paper he was writing for school. The father thought for a minute and said it would probably be easier to explain what leadership is not. He went on to say that "leadership" is not power, position, privilege, status, authority, or control. His son thought about this for a few minutes and told his dad he could have all that leadership stuff. He said he would rather have power, position, status, and control. *How would you have responded?*

▶ Leaders often have the following:

- Position, that is misused authority.
- Power, that is abused for control.
- Privilege, that profits from pleasures.

▶ Leaders often possess power, position, and privilege along with ethical principles. Let's see what's different:

- Strength and compassion are joined, libertating others.
- Severity is balanced with gentleness.
- Patience is balanced with decisiveness.

▶ Leadership is not awarded, appointed, or assigned—rather, leadership is earned:

- The true measure of leadership is influence.
- Influence is getting the other person to participate willingly.

▶ Leadership is not being distant and impersonal:

Warren Bennis has observed, "Distant and impersonal leaders are like pornographic film stars, a pretend closeness of relationship and love while removed from responsibility, accountability, and gult." (1989). Workplace pornography is being out of touch with people, customers, and employees and becoming insulated by position, power, money, and circumstances from what is really going on.

▶ Leadership is not about selfishness and personal gain.

Neglect of service is indicative of a society that is becoming more self-centered. A self-centered society is one that is committed to being and getting rather than giving.

In chapter 2 of *Ethical Leadership,* six basic principles of ethical leadership are provided. They are the following:

PRINCIPLE 1:   Caring for others is the first step toward ethical leadership.

PRINCIPLE 2:   Recognizing the dignity and worth of those with whom you work and serve by putting every educator, student, and staff member on an equal human level.

PRINCIPLE 3:   Becoming a positive force for improving the human value within your workplace.

PRINCIPLE 4:   Leading from character and with confidence and self-respect, which are the necessary first steps for personal and organizational improvement.

PRINCIPLE 5:   Making creative change the norm by letting go of the old and leading on the edge of possibility.

PRINCIPLE 6:   Committing oneself to open communication and dialogue by including others in planning, initiating, and decision making processes.

Take time to review these principles and use them as a foundation for completing activity 5 on the next page. By this time students should be able to complete the activity without hesitation, in easily understood words. For example, when activity 5 has been completed the teacher might ask, "So, what is the difference between good and bad leaders?" Students should answer, "Leaders who espouse ethical values."

Remember:

No tool can help the leader who lacks self-knowledge, and no leader can help others who are not helping them know themselves.

Activity 5: Good and Bad Leaders

Question: If we need to follow leaders who espouse ethical values, maybe we should first try to identify those characteristics and values that make one ethical, moral, or good as opposed to nonethical, immoral, and bad. Below, list what you think are the ethical characteristics required of effective leadership; then provide reasons for following the ethical leader as opposed to the nonethical one.

Ethical Characteristics:

_____

_____

_____

_____

_____

_____

_____

Reasons for Following:

_____

_____

_____

_____

_____

_____

_____

CONCEPT 1.2
Leaders lead from the inside out.

Purpose:

The purpose of concept 1.2 is to establish: "We always project on the outside what we think on the inside; therefore, we lead from the inside out!"

Procedures:

- Put concept 1.2 on the board or on an overhead. Ask the class to join you in an open discussion about its meaning and importance. Bring into this discussion what was learned in activities 1–5. This makes a natural summary for this section.

- Summarize the major points made by students during the above discussion and then go to the section entitled, "What Do Followers Expect from Their Leaders?" Discuss this page with students before completing activity 6.

- Students should now be ready to complete activity 6. When they have completed this activity, ask them to share some of their statements with the entire class. It is natural that others will ask questions and engage each other in discussions about their answers.

- Complete the analysis of concept 1.2 with a discussion of the sections "How Leaders Perceive Themselves," "Five Timeless Disciplines of Leadership," and "Things to Remember."

People in organizations are primarily looking for meaning in their work. But not many leaders act as though they believe that's what really motivates people. They think money motivates people. At the end of the day, people want to know they've done something meaningful.—Bill George

WHAT DO FOLLOWERS EXPECT FROM THEIR LEADERS?

National surveys consistently reinforce the fact that the top four values followers expect from their leaders are the following:

▸ Integrity—"I do what I say and tell the truth."
▸ Competence—"I know what I'm talking about, yet I'm willing to learn."
▸ Forward Looking—"I know where I'm going, and I've made my decisions with empathy for those I lead.
▸ Inspiration—"I'm excited about it, and I want you with me."

The eleven remaining values from the survey were being intelligent, fair-minded, broadminded, courageous, straightforward, positive, dependable, supportive, controlled, loyal, and independent.

It is not to find better values, but to be faithful to the ones we profess.—John Gardner

REASONS LEADERS ARE FOLLOWED

(Alternative ways of presenting expectations of followers)

Character:	Who we are
Relationships:	Who we know
Knowledge:	What we know
Intuition:	What we feel
Experience:	Where we have been
Past Successes:	What we have done
Ability:	What we can do

One method of teaching the concepts in the preceding box is to write them on the board and ask students to discuss the connections between each pair. Have them brainstorm as many connections as they can think of between relationships and the reasons they are connected.

Activity 6: Values You Prefer in Great Leaders

Directions: List the values you prefer in great leaders and give reasons for each value/behavior that you list.

Values You Prefer in Famous Leaders or Leaders You Have Known:	Provide Reasons for Each Value That You List:

HOW LEADERS PERCEIVE THEMSELVES

1. Leaders perceive themselves as leaders.

Leaders choose to lead and in so doing commit themselves to a journey of lifelong learning and thinking.

2. Leaders develop perceptions of themselves by carefully and realistically analyzing their lives.

Analyzing yourself means separating who you are and who you want to be from what the world thinks you are and wants you to be—your inner-self from your perceived *persona*.

It also means analyzing your strengths and weaknesses and the ability to handle both self-evaluations and those of others.

Ignorance about yourself is self-imposed and potentially limiting.

The purpose of analysis is to make the unconscious conscious.—Sigmund Freud

3. Leaders develop a strong self-image by conquering the inner foes of self-doubt, fear, and insecurity.

Self-confidence is not self-centeredness; you become self-confident by losing self in order to invest in others.

4. Leaders approve of themselves.

Self-esteem is a gift. It is knowing you don't have a limit placed on you by someone else.

We always project on the outside how we feel on the inside.

SUMMARY

FIVE TIMELESS DISCIPLINES OF LEADERSHIP

1. **It's about CHANGE:** Leadership is embracing change because the behaviors, attitudes, and methods that were responsible for success in the past will probably not be acceptable for the future.

   We live in a moment in time where the rate of change is so speeded up, we see the future only as it is disappearing.—R. D. Laing

   The chief job of leaders at all levels is to oversee the dismantling of old truths and prepare people and organizations to deal with, to love, to develop affection for change as innovations are proposed, tested, ejected, and adopted —Tom Peters

2. **It's about UNITY:** Leadership is getting people to buy into shared values, purpose, and mission; at the same time, it is about creating, communicating, and bringing into reality a vision of the future that in some way is better than the present.

   We must have stability of purpose in order to deal with instability of environment.—Tom

   Peters

3. **It's about TRANSFORMATION:** Leadership is being a competent and personal learner, gaining new knowledge resulting in new insights. Leadership is creating a learning environment to reinforce a commitment to continuous growth, development, and improvement, which results in growing other leaders.

   The illiterate of the future are not those who cannot read or write, but those who cannot learn, unlearn, and relearn.—Alvin Toffler

4. **It's about RELATIONSHIPS:** Leadership is empowering people by giving them a sense of significance and commitment rather than compliance. Leaders bring out the best in others because their belief in others creates a self-fulfilling prophecy: we do as we are expected to do. It is loving people and serving people, and recognizing that personal success is dependent upon the success of others. Everybody is going to serve somebody or something.

A leader is a follower is a leader.—Gertrude Stein

5. **It's about PERFORMANCE:** Leadership is managing yourself, walking your talk, challenging the process, and continually improving. This is the golden rule of leadership. Leaders perceive themselves as leaders and become satisfied with themselves. You don't become a leader, you become yourself, capitalizing on and improving your skills, gifts, talents, and energies (Bennis, 1989).

What you do shouts so loud that what you say isn't always heard.—Ralph Waldo Emerson

Summary:

- Leadership is extremely complex.
- Leadership cannot be taught, it must be learned.
- Leadership is always under construction.
- Your ability to build is determined by the strength of your foundation.

THINGS TO REMEMBER

- Nothing happens until someone provides leadership for it to happen; therefore, everything rises and falls on leadership.

- There is no one way to lead.

- Leadership cannot be taught; it must be learned and the moment you stop learning, you stop leading.

- Leadership is not power, position, or control, but influence.

- Leadership that is divorced from ethics is reduced to mere technique.

- Times change, technologies move forward, cultures vary, and personal agendas are diverse, but the principles of leadership are constant and will stand the test of time.

Character: The Foundation of Leadership

CONCEPT 1.3
Character is the foundation of leadership and character is always under construction.

Purpose:

In section 1 we learned that values, beliefs, and purposes support the major motifs or functions of leadership. The purpose of section 2 is to focus attention on those three motifs as tools for character building.

Procedures:

- Discuss concept 1.3 with the class. Through discussion find out what the students think it means.

- Use the material, "What Is Character?" as a foundation for this discussion and conclude with the questions for discussion below.

- Assign chapter 3 of *Ethical Leadership*. After this chapter has been read, engage students in activities 5–8 that appear at the end of that chapter.

- Conclude your discussion of concept 1.3 with activity 7. The purpose of this activity is to have students summarize their personal values, beliefs, and purposes that are the foundation of their character. Special note: Students will necessarily be hesitant, vague, and perhaps stumble a bit during these discussions and activities. That's okay, for the purpose of this section is to help them get in touch with their inner selves, which is a very difficult task for all of us.

Questions for Discussion:

[Start this section with activity 7 and use the questions below to stimulate student responses.]

- What is character? (The will to do what's right regardless of the consequences or the cost.)

- Why should I want to be a person of character? (One word—relationships! Can I have sustainable relationships void of ethical behavior?)

- What do I get from being a person of character? (It's not what you get that is important but what you are becoming through the relationships you are able to sustain.)

- Why are we more concerned about the character of others than we are about our own character?

What Is Character? A Discussion

According to Kevin Cashman (*Leadership from the Inside Out,* 1998, and Peter Senge, *Fifth Discipline,* 1990), character is about "growth toward wholeness." It is about appreciating our strengths and developing the undeveloped sides of us. It is leadership that stems from our values and beliefs, transformed into purpose and mission. Cashman comments, "Character is the essence, the being of the leader, which is deeper and broader than any action or achievement. It is the essential nature of the person. . . . The purpose of character is to transform and to open up possibilities and potentialities. Qualities of character include authenticity, purpose, openness, trust, congruence, compassion, and creating value." (31–43)

From Cashman we learn that there are ethical overtones to "character." The person of ethical character is a person who . . .

- Affirms the worth, dignity, and the uniqueness of every human being.

- Uses reason, compassion, and responsibility in decision making and problem solving.

- Works with others to improve our world and the world of our children.

- Believes that human life is most meaningful when lived by ethical principles.

Example:

The following example illustrates quite vividly the concept of "ethical character" as applied to an entire corporation: John Allison IV is a businessman-philosopher and CEO of BB&T Corporation, a bank with its own philosophical standards. In fact, according to *The Charlotte Observer,* Monday, December 20, 1999, the beliefs, values, and purposes of BB&T are fast becoming a mainstay of axioms for southern banking.

The core *values* and *definitions* of BB&T, as espoused by Allison, are the following:

1. **REALITY:** If we want to be better, we must act within the context of reality.

2. **REASON:** Mankind has a specific means of survival, which is the ability to think.

3. **INDEPENDENT THINKING:** All employees are challenged to use their individual minds to their optimum to make rational decisions.

4. **PRODUCTIVITY:** We are committed to being producers of wealth and well-being by taking actions necessary to accomplish our mission.

5. **HONESTY:** Being honest is simply being consistent with reality.

6. **INTEGRITY:** Regardless of the short-term benefits, acting inconsistently with our principles is to our long-term detriment.

7. **JUSTICE:** Individuals should be evaluated and rewarded objectively, based on their contributions toward accomplishing our mission.

8. **PRIDE:** Pride is the psychological reward we earn from living by our values; i.e., from being just, honest, and having integrity.

9. **SELF-ESTEEM:** We expect our employees to earn positive self-esteem from doing their work well.

10. **TEAMWORK:** While independent thought and strong personal goals are very important, our work is accomplished within teams.

WHAT WE HAVE LEARNED

1. Character is the will to do what is *right* regardless of the consequences or the costs. It is doing what is right because it is right, not because I'm afraid of getting caught doing wrong.

2. Character is what I think, and because what I think changes with learning and experience, *character is always under construction.* The primary means by which character is developed and transformed is a continuous process of renewing how we think, because we are what we think! Also, what we think is determined by what we experience and by those people and situations to which we are exposed.

3. Values, beliefs, and purpose are the foundation and tools of character transformation and renewal. This is a difficult task and will take place over time because it requires that we shed many of our old beliefs and habits and take on new ones.

4. Character development comes with a price. Why? In our society it seems that it is more important what I do or feel than who I am. "Therefore, we become more concerned about achievement and/or fulfillment than character. When we pursue achievement and/or fulfillment (what I do or how I feel) over character, we introduce a new value into our lives, which tells us that whatever advances achievement or fulfillment is *right* and anything that hinders achievement or fulfillment is *wrong*" (Andy Stanley, *Like a Rock, Becoming a Person of Character*, New York: Thomas Nelson, 1997).

5. Character is the lubricant of relationships. Consider the following: When the lubricant of character is missing from a relationship, the relationship eventually breaks down and is destroyed, bit-by-bit. Ethical character not only builds relationships but keeps them maintained over the bumps and potholes of everyday living. When character takes a backseat to achievement and/or fulfillment there will always be a breakdown of relationships because the essential bond between individuals (honesty, integrity, fair play, and honor) is missing.

IN SUMMARY: Show me an organization, team, school, or business where achievement and fulfillment have been chosen over character and I will show you broken relationships and the inability of a leader or leaders to lead—therefore,

> leadership from the inside out is the application of character.

Activity 7: Touchstones of Character

Directions: Before proceeding with our discussion of *character,* we need to spend some time thinking and brainstorming ideas and qualities about ourselves—ideas and qualities that make up our characters. Because character is made up of our beliefs, values, and purposes, use these concepts as the broad categories for describing your own character.

Put your name at the top of the graphic. Then list your character traits under the classification categories provided. Make these your most significant qualities that best define who you are. In order to use this visual successfully, return to the discussion questions starting on page 22 and ask them of yourself. Then, review the above information on character. When your review has been completed, finish the following activity. Finally, *circle* those character traits that you believe need further clarification and/or modification.

For Your Information:

Values are the characteristics by which we are known.

Beliefs are the foundation of values and purposes. Beliefs apply the moral qualities that determine the way we think, feel, and behave in the important matters of life.

Purpose is the goal, object, or end for which something is made, used, or initiated.

Your Name

Values	Beliefs	Purpose
_____	_____	_____
_____	_____	_____
_____	_____	_____
_____	_____	_____
_____	_____	_____
_____	_____	_____
_____	_____	_____
_____	_____	_____

CONCEPT 1.4

Character construction requires tools. If you don't make the tool selection your choice, someone or something else will make the choice for you.

Purpose:

The purpose of this section is to discover the importance of personally defining and developing values, beliefs, and purpose for building and maintaining character, the character of oneself and the organization of which you are a part.

Remember:

- Values are the characteristics by which we are known.

- Beliefs are the foundation of values and purposes. Beliefs apply the moral qualities that determine the way we think, feel, and behave in the important matters of life.

- Purpose is the goal, object, or end for which something is made, used, or initiated.

Procedures:

- Discuss concept 1.4 with the class. Through discussion find out what the students think it means.

Activities:

1. Review the graphic on the next pages. Point out the importance of values, beliefs, and purpose for character building.

2. Review the value examples provided under the heading "Values." Ask the class to add to this list and write them on the board. Use this list to complete activity 8.

3. Complete the section on values by asking the question: "Will values change with time?" Point out to students that values will change and this can sometimes be a positive opportunity in their development.

4. Read Cashman's statement about beliefs (page 22) to the class or put it on an overhead. Discuss its meaning in small groups and share various meanings and interpretations with the entire class.

5. Complete activity 9. ("Belief Examples" are provided as a starting point.)

6. Ask: "Why do I need a life purpose?" Record and discuss class responses. Go over additional responses found in this section.

7. Share major points on defining "purpose" and have class read the "Earthquake Story." When read, they are to relate its meaning to the development of a life purpose and share their understandings with the entire class. Complete this discussion by sharing "Four Ways to Create a Life Purpose." Students should be encouraged to evaluate themselves and tell where they believe their purpose originates.

8. Ask students to give their reactions to Mary Tribble's comments. Use the questions and possible answers (under heading: "Purpose Will Answer the Following Two Questions") prior to engaging students in activity 10. Then complete activity 10.

9. Have students use activities 8–10 as a foundation for writing a mission statement. Remind them that a mission statement is a roadmap for completing their purpose. Complete activity 11.

10. Conclude this section by having students review activities 7–11 and complete the summary chart "Character Is the Foundation of Leadership."

11. Complete activity 12 and discuss.

12. Review with "Things to Remember."

THREE BASIC BUILDING BLOCKS OF CHARACTER

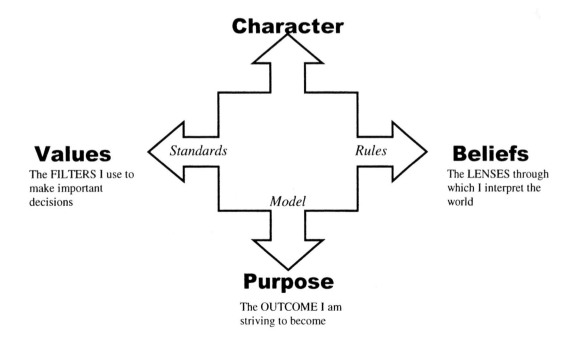

VALUES

Values are the qualities/moral fiber by which I am known; the means by which I make decisions, evaluate successes, and learn from failures. Values identify who I am, on the inside.

We must see resurgence in the importance of values. We must narrow the gap between what we believe and how we act. There must be a commitment to a set of higher beliefs rather than our own narrow interest.—Michael Annison

VALUE EXAMPLES:

POSITIVE

Integrity, trustworthiness, honesty, vision, forward thinking, competence, inspiring, enthusiastic, loyalty, responsibility, accountability, just, capability, effectiveness, teachable, wise, creditable, compassionate, consistent, reliable, adaptable, flexible, loving, patient, decisive, passionate, encouraging, faithful, confident, quality, sincere, guileless, courageous, straightforwardness, positive, dependable, self-control, excellence, unselfish, courteous, humble, gracious, tolerant, obedient, boldness, forgiving, discerning, joyfulness, diligence, endurance, creative, truthful, and disciplined.

NEGATIVE

Selfish, jealous, deceit, manipulation, greed, immoral, controlling, power hungry, distant, impersonal, corrupt, lying, cheating, arrogant.

Activity 8: Defining Important Values

1. Depending on how the class is organized—as a class, group, or as an individual, select ten values that you consider important and list below:

1. _____

2. _____

3. _____

4. _____

5. _____

6. _____

7. _____

8. _____

9. _____

10. _____

2. From these ten values, select five you consider the most important and prioritize them the most important (1) to the least important (5):

1. _____

2. _____

3. _____

4. _____

5. _____

3. Using class discussion and dialogue, define each of these values and provide an example of each of them:

1. _____

2. _____

3. _____

4. _____

5. _____

BELIEFS

Beliefs are a state of mind in which trust and confidence are placed in some person, some thing, or some being. According to Kevin Cashman, "Beliefs literally create our reality; they are the lenses through which we interpret the world. Also, beliefs are transformational. Every belief we have transforms our life in either a life-enriching or life-limiting way."

THE ORIGIN OF OUR BELIEFS

• Our beliefs may originate in a higher being found at the apex of a religion, which sets the standards for conduct and living. These are our "Moral Footprints."

• Some beliefs may be in you, another person, or a religious being. A lesson learned from history is that human character is greatly influenced by one's environment. As cultural forces change, we are changed as well. It is important that our beliefs remain stable as the world around us changes.

• We know that opposing worldviews tend to move people apart. Common ground for ethics and morality (our "Moral Footprints") are difficult to discern, especially when we are unwilling or unable to understand the point(s) of others.

• Beliefs are transformational. They are either life-enriching or life-limiting. *Life-enriching* beliefs are conscious beliefs that build character and focused leadership. They originate from inside of us and are seen in what we do and how we treat others.

• On the other hand, *life-limiting* beliefs are usually unconscious (shadow beliefs) that create superficial leadership behaviors. They block our inner self from others, and, maybe, from our own conscious evaluation. For example, we may say that we desire that decisions be made at the level where there is firsthand knowledge of situations and problems; but we really want subordinates to do what we say and feel that we are always right, can't let go of power, and believe in success at all costs. This means that our beliefs include power, control, self-interest, and pride of position. Even though we say that others should lead at their level of expertise, we have these unconscious, shadow beliefs that limit our leadership to micromanaging, which creates disharmony and distrust in the ability of others.

• Finally, we need to examine the excuses we use to explain or rationalize behaviors based on these unconscious beliefs. These may include, but are not limited to, the following:

    ▪ "I can't help it!"
    ▪ "Who's going to know?"
    ▪ "He/she/they deserve it."
    ▪ "I deserve it and need it."
    ▪ "I only did it once."
    ▪ "It's their fault!"

- What we should understand is that beliefs shape our attitudes and influence our actions. As long as we believe incorrectly, how is it possible to improve our character?

- Further, we need more understanding about the following:

  - What I believe about myself.
  - What I believe about others.
  - What I believe about life.
  - What I believe about learning and growth.
  - What I believe about my leaders.

Chapter 3 of *Ethical Leadership* provides an analysis of the trust structures needed for any effective organization, group, department, family, etc. Before these trust structures are discussed, Dr. Hester provides a set of beliefs, which form the foundation of trusting. Consider the following: Leaders are responsible for developing strong commitments to the mission and purposes of learning and strong beliefs that structure, support, and communicate them throughout the educational organization. From these commitments and beliefs are built the trusting relationships that sustain productive school systems. They emanate from our beliefs about persons, such as the following:

1. Individuals can live and work harmoniously through combining personal satisfaction and self-development with significant work and other activities that contribute to the welfare of the family, school, and community.

2. Individuals will develop faith in others if we have faith in them; they can tap their own power to solve difficult problems if we teach them to reason and share their responses.

3. A person's uniqueness will unfold quite naturally as we express respect for her or his abilities as well as possibilities.

4. Each person possesses intrinsic moral and intellectual worth and we should look upon each individual, as well as ourselves, as natural and good.

5. We do not have to grow at the expense of others. This means that each of us has the ability to reach out creatively beyond our own physical and mental boundaries and maintain ethical consistency and integrity in our lives.

6. Individuals are naturally open and responsive to their environment. Therefore, we must invite them to discuss their ideas, share their values, and model growth-producing ethical behaviors.

7. Finally, individuals are naturally creative and curious and the more they learn and practice intellectually and ethically, the more abundantly they will produce for themselves and for their families and communities.

TRY THIS: Examine each of these beliefs. (1) In your own words, very simply restate the belief statement, (2) provide two or three reasons why you agree or disagree with each of these beliefs, and (3) are there other beliefs about persons that you would like to add? Add these to the list.

BELIEF EXAMPLES

Beliefs can be divided into many categories. Basic among these are religion, family, and career. Others include one's nation, school, or some other organization such as teams, clubs, or civic groups. Here are several examples (use these in activity #8 that follows):

Religion

- Belief in a higher being

- Belief in organized religion

- Belief in an afterlife

- Belief that our morals are established in religion and provide standards for living

- Others:

_____

_____

_____

_____

Relationships

- Belief that we are accountable to our friends and family and owe them our stewardship

- Belief that we are responsible to our friends and family

- Belief in the sanctity of the home; the sanctity of personal relationships

- Belief that family and friends provide security, empowerment, and peace of mind

- Belief that commitment to friends and family are the cornerstones of society

- Belief in the value of friendship

- Others:

_____

_____

_____

_____

Career

- Belief that career demands our excellence, commitment, and responsibility

- Belief that we should be dependable and loyal employees

- Belief that in our decision making we should be patient and achieve balance, even in the face of diversity

- Belief in our continual education and learning

- Belief in the veracity of fellow workers

- Others:

_____

_____

_____

_____

Activity 9: Defining Personal Beliefs

1. In groups of 3–5, discuss your foundational beliefs and select what you consider to be the five most important:

1. _____

2. _____

3. _____

4. _____

5. _____

2. From this group of five beliefs, discuss the importance of each, then select those you consider to be the top three and rank them in order of importance:

1. _____

2. _____

3. _____

3. Choose three different words that share the meaning of each belief in 2 above:

Belief 1: _____

_____

_____

Belief 2: _____

_____

_____

Belief 3: _____

_____

_____

Purpose

Until thought is linked to purpose, there is no intelligent accomplishment.—James Allen, *As Man Thinketh*

Why Do I Need a Life Purpose?

- It forces me to make a choice.

- It lets others know where I stand and sets the stage for the demands of external influences.

- It helps me to better determine what is important and what is not important.

- It releases my power of conviction, commitment, and determination.

- It is the foundation of my vision, my single most important motivator.

Purpose is the model of who and what I am striving to become—the "Gold" Medal of life. Life's purpose is a reflection of one's fundamental values and beliefs. We are what we think, and what we think is determined by what we experience. That which we experience is determined by that to which we have been exposed.

Life's purpose is both a road map and a compass. It gives meaning to life and defines why we are here, doing what we are doing, and believing what we believe. Purpose is the foundation for a new way of life and it is not only a question of character but of legacy as well. That is, legacy is about longevity and what you do consistently over the long haul.

PURPOSE IS EXTREMELY IMPORTANT BECAUSE:

- Purpose defines our decision making.

- Purpose determines how we understand and handle new problems.

- Lack of purpose disables one's motivation and courage to rise above the moment.

- A strong purpose keeps us focused and enables our creativity and flexibility.

PURPOSE HAS THREE DIMENSIONS:

- Ultimate purpose is those values, beliefs, and practices we are unwilling to give up.

- Unique purpose is that which defines who you are; that which is unique to you.

- Unity of purpose brings ultimate and unique purposes together, which creates unity in oneself and in the organizations to which we belong. It means working toward the same goals in a harmonious environment.

Earthquake Story

The following story tells us that *purpose* must be both stable and flexible:

How many of you have experienced an earthquake? I will never forget my first earthquake experience. My family and I had moved to northern California and I had opened a new office in San Mateo. It was located in a beautiful office park in the hills overlooking Foster City and the San Francisco Bay. It was a typical hillside California building where half of the building was connected to land and the other half was sitting on stilts.

One afternoon at about two o'clock, I was sitting at my desk talking to a customer and, with no warning, it was as if a giant came and stood over our building, placing his hands on each end with the intent of shaking things up. Needless to say, more than my desk and bookshelves were shaken up. I immediately jumped up to run when it dawned on me that there was no place to go. I had been told that when there was an earthquake; stand under a doorway for protection. I did, but standing there did not give me a lot of comfort.

What I experienced next was the most amazing sight I had ever witnessed. I began to see the side of our building, which was all glass, begin to bevel as if it were overheated transparency film. All I could think of was broken glass flying everywhere. However, to my surprise, not one section of the glass broke and the building did not suffer any damage. My desk was overturned, books and papers were scattered over the floor, and our computer room was in shambles. This was my first earthquake experience, but, unfortunately, it was not my last.

Several months passed and our company had outgrown its space. I was in the process of contracting for additional space in a building down the street when I ran into the contractor while walking about the building trying to decide what floor we wanted for our offices. After discussing which offices had the best view of the bay (a critical topic in California), I asked him to explain how this building could withstand an earthquake like the one we had experienced several months ago. "First," he said, "We have to dig down, regardless of how far, until we hit bedrock. That gives us the stability we need for our foundation. Second, we use many different sizes and strengths of steel and we tie them in many different ways to give our foundation flexibility. You see, we need a strong foundation in order to allow the steel to give and sway as the earth moves around and under the concrete pillars." I looked at him for a second and said, "Let me make sure I understand. You're saying that in order for this building not to fall during an earthquake it must have both stability and flexibility." "That's right; stable, yet flexible."

You must have stability of purpose in order to deal with instability of environment.—Tom Peters

PURPOSE IS A CALL TO SERVICE:

- Purpose is discovered in service because purpose adds value to others.

- Purpose is about human growth, especially growth in building relationships with others.

  As relationships are strengthened, we grow as persons. It is a push and pull situation—we push our ethical behaviors toward others and at the same time; pull the strength of their character toward us. When others do the same, the relationship becomes grounded in the strength of both characters.

> **PURPOSE IS A MAJOR CORNERSTONE OF LEADERSHIP AND LEADERSHIP IS EXPRESSING OUR TALENTS AND SKILLS IN THE SERVICE OF OTHERS. THE PURPOSE OF LEADERSHIP IS SERVICE.**

Purpose is constant throughout life; it is the manifestation of purpose that is always changing.—
H. Darrell Young

REMEMBER, PURPOSE IS ALWAYS BECOMING:

- Too often our purpose gets defined as a result of what we do; therefore, who we are becomes controlled by external circumstances and our purpose becomes overshadowed by the events of our lives.

- When stating your purpose, always value who you are over what you do, but do what you do to the best of your ability.

- What you do, where you do it, how you do it, and with whom you do it will have an impact on what you become; that is, on your purpose.

PURPOSE AND MISSION:

Never confuse purpose with mission. Becoming (purpose) must always take precedence over doing; yet we must always do the best that our ability allows. Many organizations require departments to develop mission statements. On too many occasions, mission statements are developed without any idea as to the organization's purpose. But purpose determines and drives the mission of the organization. Purpose comes first; then from purpose, we should be able to develop the strategies for carrying out the organization's purpose. These strategies comprise the organization's (or departments within an organization) mission statement. Mission is doing! Keep in mind the following;

- Mission is what we do, an event, a project.

- Mission is a question of how we're equipped.

- Missions are the steps to achieving purpose.

- Forces that we have no control over can impact missions.

- We need to choose missions that fit our preparation, emotion, and abilities.

- Missions change as we change.

Mary Tribble, CEO of a special events production company observes that the "significance of the human element is re-gaining strength." She says, "With so much emphasis placed on knowledge over product, companies are slowly awakening to the weight of their employees' worth. A few are beginning to understand that their employees' individual fulfillment will lead to the success of the collective whole."

Wonderfully, she observes, "Individual achievement is invariably linked with one's inner purpose. It's the ability to know one's destination and to spend each day carefully laying footstones to get there. This is not about setting career or monetary goals; it's about understanding the larger contribution one is meant to make, and arranging one's life and career to deliver the goods."

Finally, she comments, "We are all here to fulfill a purpose, and that purpose is rarely completely in synch with our job descriptions. But it can be in harmony with them, if we have a clear vision of how we relate to the exterior world (*The Charlotte Observer*, Tuesday, January 4, 2000).

FOUR WAYS TO CREATE A LIFE PURPOSE

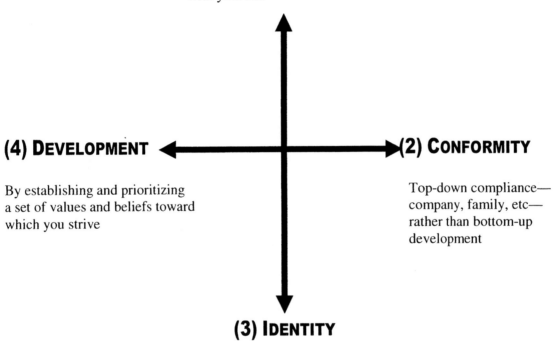

(1) ANALYSIS

Toward the end of life you add up the score-card and determine what you did with your life

(4) DEVELOPMENT

By establishing and prioritizing a set of values and beliefs toward which you strive

(2) CONFORMITY

Top-down compliance—company, family, etc—rather than bottom-up development

(3) IDENTITY

Heroes after whom you have patterned your life

PURPOSE WILL ANSWER THE FOLLOWING
TWO QUESTIONS

1. What I am striving to become?

2. How will I achieve it?

POSSIBLE ANSWERS:

- Continuous learning, growth, and improvement

- Learning to lead by following good leaders

- Live by an authority greater than self

- Be in control of what I experience, when, and where

- Demonstrate personal leadership

- Self-control and discipline

- Behaviors that reflect my values and beliefs

- Treat others like I want to be treated

- Lead a moral and ethical life

- Increasing knowledge, understanding, and wisdom

- Live a responsible and accountable life

- Being an effective listener, open-minded, and one who seeks to empower others

- Being an agent of change and having a willingness to be taught

- Behaviors that speak so loud that my words are always heard

- Learning to be wise, developing good judgment, and common sense

- Being a catalyst for personal awakening

- Helping others help themselves to become leaders

- Growth through change, stewardship, and responsibility

NOTE: Use these or other ideas to complete activity 10.

Students should understand that the idea of the self is intrinsically bound to purpose: the idea of self emerges only when we—and our communities of interest, family, and work—begin to feel solidly secure about our future as a whole. Although the idea of "purpose" seems obsolete in our consumer-fed society, many today are voicing a yearning to recapture the dynamic of mutual help that so typifies family and village life in days gone by. We should perhaps understand that purpose, as a definition of the "self," is stronger and more alive when drawn from within, but, ironically, functions best when supported and served by the group(s) with whom we live and work.

It is purpose that that carries civilization forward. Leaders with purpose understand that they are standing on the edge of something; and that knowledge, that certainty set them somehow apart as leaders others aspire to follow. A leader with a clear sense of purpose has a view that is somehow much larger than one person, a view that encompasses the future with a desire to change it for the better. Understanding "purpose" is acknowledging, "Ideas live in people." Only when leaders translate their purposes into concrete realities and with understanding, and only when the ideas of leaders are given to those who need them are their deeper meanings revealed. Purpose, clearly articulated and patiently transmitted through word and deed, represents the wisdom of the organization, its foundation, and its future.

Activity 10: Constructing a Purpose Statement

1. Review your values, beliefs, and your thoughts on your personal purpose. From these choose a minimum of five words or phrases that describe what you are striving to become:

EXAMPLES:

1. More committed to my work.

2. Dedicated to leadership improvement.

3. More organized.

4. More disciplined and consistent.

5. More focused on personal development.

YOUR CHOICES:

1. _____

2. _____

3. _____

4. _____

5. _____

2. Write a *purpose* statement using the words that you have chosen as your foundation:

EXAMPLE:

My purpose is commitment to continuous growth and development that reflect the behavior of a leader blended with the discipline of a manager.

OR

My purpose is to become a leader who will strive to develop personal abilities and the abilities of others.

YOUR PURPOSE STATEMENT:

_____

_____

_____

_____

_____

_____

SUMMARY:
CHARACTER IS THE FOUNDATION OF LEADERSHIP

Directions: Summarize your values, beliefs, and purpose in the left-hand column. In the right hand column, justify (that is, give reasons for) your choices.

Name: _____   Date: _____

Values	Justification
Beliefs - - - - - - - - - -	- - - - - - - - - - - - -
Purpose - - - - - - - - -	- - - - - - - - - - - - -

Activity 11: Mission Statement

Directions: From your values, beliefs, and purpose create a mission statement that pulls from all of these areas and correctly defines the direction in which you wish to take your life (school, organization, department, etc.).

MISSION STATEMENT:

Activity 12: Strategies for Implementing Mission

Directions: Create strategies for implementing the purpose of your organization/department, etc.

Strategy Steps:

1. _____

   _____

2. _____

   _____

3. _____

   _____

4. _____

   _____

5. _____

   _____

6. _____

   _____

7. _____

   _____

8. _____

   _____

9. _____

   _____

10. _____

    _____

THINGS TO REMEMBER

- Character is the will to do what is right regardless of the consequences.

- Character is the foundation of leadership; therefore, we lead from the inside out.

- Values and beliefs are the foundation of purpose.

- We are what we think and what we think is determined by what we experience, and what we experience is determined by what we expose ourselves to.

- Life's purpose is a call to service.

- Life purpose precedes life plans.

- Your life purpose will determine how you make life decisions.

- Your life purpose will determine how you view life's problems.

- The key to being unified without being uniform is unity of purpose.

- The effectiveness of my public leadership is determined by my private life.

Unity of Vision

CONCEPT 1.5
Trust is the primary behavior for realizing one's vision.

Purpose:

The purpose of this section is to accurately and clearly define our vision and learn how to more effectively communicate our vision.

Procedures:

* Discuss concept 1.5 with the class and ask them the value of trust in building organizational cohesion and stability.

* Review material "Defining Current Reality" before going on to activity 13.

* When the review and discussions are completed, ask students to complete activity 13.

VISIONS

What are visions and how important are they? Envisioning the future is a clear mental picture of what could be, fueled by the conviction that it should be. It is an architectural rendering of a future that is realistic, creditable, attractive, and, in some way, better than what presently exists; that is, it promises to produce more usable results. Visions are passions that evoke emotions, motivations where the mundane begins to matter, directions that become a moral compass, and purpose, which gives meaning to life. An old proverb says, "Share with me your vision and I will prophesy your future." Warren Bennis comments, "As a nation we cannot survive without virtue; it cannot progress without a common vision" (1989). And in the Old Testament we read, "Where there is no vision, the people perish." So, how important is vision? How important is it for us to define and share our vision of a way of life that is better—at least in some ways—than what presently exist? How important are visions to a leader's ability to motivate, challenge, and inspire followers to buy into his or her programs and methods? How important is it to have a unified and clearly articulate vision to building within your organization *unity without uniformity*?

The vision of things to be done may come a long time before the way of doing them becomes clear; but woe to him who distrust the vision.—Jenkins L. Jones

DEFINING CURRENT REALITY

DEFINING CURRENT REALITY IS AS IMPORTANT AS SEEING A VISION OF THE FUTURE: WALK BEFORE YOU TALK; INVESTIGATE BEFORE YOU INITIATE.

Questions:

- In what kind of atmosphere do I study? Learn?

- Who are the important people in my life?

- Given where we are today, how can we best reach our maximum potential?

- What are potential barriers to achieving my maximum potential?

- How do my friends, customers, co-workers, etc. define "value"?

- What are we doing to maximize our potential?

- How do we currently perceive our value?

- What do my friends or associates say about the atmosphere in which we work or study?

- How are things changing around us?

- What are the forces I/we can't control?

- What are our current strengths and weaknesses?

- What are our future opportunities?

- How do we/others feel about our past performance(s)?

CREATING THE VISION

1. Creating the vision means being able to see widely—the whole and its parts.

2. Creating the vision means being flexible and having the ability to change when situations require it. This takes an incredible amount of energy.

3. Creating the vision requires challenging conformity and living on the edge of possibility.

4. Creating the vision requires reasons and intuition, knowledge and understanding. It requires a problem-solving mind.

5. Vision calls forth innovation, which is built by information gathered from new connections—from ongoing circles of exchange where information is not merely accumulated and stored, but created and shared.

◀ Characteristics of Vision

- Vision honors the past.

- Vision is a significant tool for managing change.

- Vision is the essence of effective leadership.

- Vision is the single most important motivator of people.

Where we have a vision of where we wish to lead and the kind of organization we wish to create, then we act in ways that we believe are in pursuit of creating that future.—Victor Frankel, *Man's Search for Meaning*

◀ The Sources of Visions

- Visions come from a collage of knowledge, understanding, information, experiences, and exposures.

- Visions come from what we learn and observe from others.

- Visions come from our ability to listen, imagine, and picture.

- Visions come from an informed intuition—great leaders see things others can't or won't and move forward before others know what is happening.

We dare not have solitary beings. Every creature is, in some sense, connected to and dependent on the rest.—Lewis Thomas, *The Lives of a Cell*

Contexts are frameworks within which ideas can be judged.—Bob Samples, *The Metaphoric Mind*

◀ Charting the Course

- Evaluate the possible environments for the future.

- Identify the opportunities in these environments.

- Draw on past experiences for perspective, stability, and support.

- Try to view your mission and work from the point of view of others.

- See the "whole" in appropriate detail and perspective.

- Anticipate conceivable responses from others.

- Review as things change.

◀ Getting Started

- Visualize and plan the whole trip before you begin.

- Create a vision of the destination.

- Understand what it will take to get there.

- Know who you need to help get you there.

- Recognize the obstacles.

Activity 13: What Is Your Vision?

Directions: You have developed a purpose statement and mission strategies for yourself/your organization. Now is the time to rethink those statements. Activity 13 will help you do just that.

1. First, get a picture in your head of your team, group, or organization. Where is your organization now in relationship to those whom you serve: employee/student satisfaction, training, innovation, and product development, etc.?

   Answer: Where *should* your organization be in relationship to these factors? Review your answers to the questions found in this section under the heading "Defining Current Reality," and on the lines below describe your organization from your answers to the above inquiry:

   _____

   _____

   _____

   _____

   _____

   _____

2. From your written description construct a vision statement of what you would like your organization to be like in the next five to ten years. Write it on the lines below:

   _____

   _____

   _____

   _____

   _____

   _____

   _____

COMMUNICATING THE VISION AND ENLISTING OTHERS

Purpose:

Effective communication at all levels of an organization is indispensable for the development of mission clarity and the actualization of vision. This section focuses on effective communication.

Procedures:

- Review 1–3 below with the class. Complete activity 14.

- Review 4–5 below with the class. Complete activities 15–16.

- Conclude section 3 with a review of the summary.

1. The Minds of Men Are in Motion

Let me explain: The next time you are in San Francisco and you want to board a cable car that is already in motion, you don't want to run at it from right angles and try to jump on board in one wild leap. If you do, you are likely to find yourself on the ground or seriously injured. No, you run alongside the cable car, increasing your speed until you are moving at the same pace as the car and in the same direction. You then jump on board.

The minds of people, like the cable car, are in motion. They are engaged with something very different from the thought you have to present to them. You can't just jump directly at them and expect to make an effective landing. You must put yourself in their place, try to imagine what they are thinking, let your first remarks be in line with their thoughts, and follow it with another with which you know the person will easily agree. Thus, gradually, their minds reach a point where they can join yours without conflict. (from Bruce Barton, *The Man Nobody Knows,* 1928).

2. Approaches to Communicating the Vision

- Develop slogans and other means to capture the essence of your vision.

- Make the pressure to achieve positive.

- Everyone who will listen needs to know. Have formal and informal meetings and use all in-house communications.
- Communicate with passion and from the heart. The greatest inhibitors to enlisting others in the vision are lack of personal conviction, sincerity, and love for others.

- Capture the imagination. Make it vivid by using images and word pictures. Use examples that are familiar to your audience; use creditable references; talk about traditional values and appeal to common beliefs. Say the same things in different ways; use metaphors for comparison to things familiar; include everyone. Begin with the realities and relate to your vision (remember: for some people change is not easy); be positive, honest, and hopeful. Speak with emotion and passion and let others know of your beliefs and convictions. Share your vision with others.

- Remember: emotion is the key to moving people to action; therefore, they must first be moved with emotion.

Establish the urgency to change first, create the need to change, remove the rewards for present behavior, and empower people to want to change.—James Belasco, *Teaching Elephants to Dance*

One of the most important ways a leader communicates a new vision is by constantly acting on it and personifying it. Live out the values you espouse and show by the choices you make, you mean what you say.—Warren Bennis

3. Characteristics of Effective Communication

This is the *key*: People don't care how much
you know until they know how much you care.

One must not always think so much about what one should do, but rather what one should be. Our works do not ennoble us; but we must ennoble our works.—Meister Eckhart (c. 1260–1237)

- Power of expression is not determined by diction, phraseology, or style; rather, it is determined by depth of heart.

- Clarity of speech comes from commitment of purpose; therefore, know where you are heading.

- Believability comes in direct proportion to humility, genuine authority, and confidence.

- Words live forever; therefore, recognize the power of language.

- Having the truth is only half the battle; know the craft.

- Be a student of people; always know your audience. Decide whom to approach and how, and whom not to approach.

- Knowing when to speak is as important as knowing what to say.

- Simplicity is saying one thing well; therefore, know your point.

- Convey urgency yet a sense of calmness; know where your responsibility begins and ends.

- Know your enemy and your ally; never underestimate your opposition.

4. Creating an Environment for Effective and Ongoing Communication

- Convincing others:

  ▶ Determine the human resource needs for the success of the vision.

  ▶ Determine where these people are currently positioned relative to supporting the vision (disarm the opposition and let go of opponents).

  ▶ Determine how their individual purpose/vision supports the collective vision.

- Peter Block's *The Empowered Manager* (1987) examines how to build support for the vision:

  ▶ Evaluate from two dimensions:

    ▪ Agreement with the vision, and

    ▪ Trust about the way I/we operate

  ▶ Identify people according to five categories:

    ▪ **Allies:** high agreement, high trust—become the foundation of critical mass and becomes both an advocate and messenger of the vision.

    ▪ **Challengers:** low agreement, high trust:

      → Challengers have conflicting visions or no vision.

      → Challengers bring reality and practicality to our vision and plans.

      → Challengers are sometimes difficult, frustrating, but invaluable; they challenge us to get it together.

      → Challengers bring out the best in us.

    ▪ **Bedfellows:** high agreement, low to moderate trust

      → Bedfellows may have hidden agendas and don't usually tell the whole story.

→ Make sure you know where they stand and that you expect them to take action.

→ Remind them they have gone on record as supporting the vision.

→ Build trust and attempt to move them to "allies," but be careful.

- **Adversaries:** low agreement, low trust

    → Make sure they deserve the title—do not try to convert them because the more you try the stronger they get; let go of adversaries.

- **Fence-sitters:** unknown agreement, low trust

    → Fence sitters will not take a stand for or against the vision; the problem is usually doubt.

    → Find out where they stand and encourage them to take a position. Remember, they are not worth a lot of energy and they will make a decision when they feel safe. There is little you can do to influence them.

5. Important Facts about Communication

1. Communication is a process that begins when you first meet someone and continues, even after the last exchange of messages.

2. Communication is irreversible even when we try to back up and explain ourselves. No explanation can erase what has been said or done.

3. Communication is not always a good thing, but its value comes from the way it is used—it can cause pain or express warm feelings and useful facts. The goal is to learn how to communicate effectively.

4. Communication will not solve all problems. It may even cause problems as you give an honest opinion that was not expected or solicited.

5. More communication is not always better. We can talk a problem to death. One key to successful communication is to share an adequate amount of information in a skillful manner.

6. Effective communication is not simple. Many people learn to communicate skillfully because those around them have exposed them to models of such behavior. They know how to do so because they have seen effective communication in action. It is a learned behavior.

7. In communication . . .

- 25 percent will hear the message and not understand it.

- 25 percent will hear the message and receive it, but not act upon it.

- 25 percent will hear the message but go in a different direction.

- 25 percent will hear the message and act to bring the vision to life.

6. Healthy Organizations Communicate Upward

From the *Orlando Sentinel* reported by Harry Wessel: *

- Stifling the concerns of workers can jeopardize a company, no matter the size.

- Communication is the lifeblood of any organization.

- Large companies and organizations that communicate effectively often mimic small companies in that employees are encouraged to give or ask for information.

- It's not enough to have policies and mission statements; upward communication has to be constantly fostered and reinforced so people see it's something that is valued and it eventually becomes natural.

- The key to effective communication in any organization is the behavior of those in decision-making positions, starting at the top.

- The most powerful solutions are the informal ones.

- Let each employee know, "I belong here. My input is valued."

- Managers and leaders must walk the walk—they must be good role models, making it clear through their behavior that they are open to information, whether positive or negative.

- Companies and organizations can foster the tendency of persons to do the right thing by creating a culture where every employee feels a part of the team and a responsibility to promote the success of the company/organization.

- Companies and organizations that are driven by a values orientation are more likely to have open communication, but those values must be reinforced by the actions of company/organizational leaders.

- Senior leaders are often the ones getting the least personal feedback; therefore, they must send signals that encourage internal and external information about the organization.

- Ultimately, communication is about the behaviors of leaders.

*See: "Lesson from Columbia Shuttle Disaster, Healthy Companies Communicate Upward, "Harry Wessel, *The Charlotte Observer,* Monday, March 24, 2003, 7D.

Activity 14: Communicating Your Vision

Directions:

1. Under the following three headings, describe three incidents in which you communicated each of the following social needs:
   - *Inclusion:* the desire to become involved with others
   - *Control:* the ability to influence others
   - *Affection:* the dimension of caring for those whom we value and have them view us as important as well.
2. Discuss these responses in small groups and gather insights from others to improve your communication skills.

Inclusion:

_____

_____

_____

_____

_____

Control:

_____

_____

_____

_____

Affection:

_____

_____

_____

_____

_____

Activity 15: Communicating Your Vision

Directions: In the following activity you will brainstorm ways you can communicate your vision throughout your organization and/or to your clients/customers. When completed, move to activity 16, and compare and contrast your ideas with the six points presented on pages 54–58.

Brainstorm: In the middle circle write two words that summarize your organization's vision. In the outer circle list as many ways you can think of (no holds barred) to communicate your organization's vision. In the outer box brainstorm and list barriers that must be overcome in order to communicate your organization's vision.

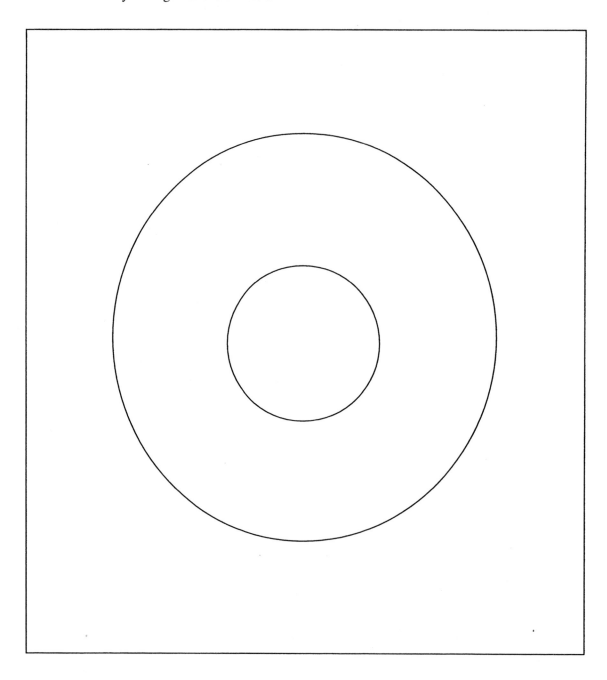

Activity 16: Communicating Your Vision

Compare and Contrast: When you have completed the brainstorming activity, compare and contrast your strategies with those on the previous pages.

- Place your strategies in the right-hand box. Summarize those strategies from this manual and put them in the left-hand box. In the middle box, put the strategies that you both share in common.

- In the space provided, list a set of strategies from all three boxes that will work for you.

STRATEGIES FROM THIS MANUAL	COMMON STRATEGIES	YOUR STRATEGIES

List strategies from above that will work for you:

_____

_____

_____

_____

_____

_____

_____

_____

SUMMARY

1. The vision will need to be challenged; current and future changes will have to be taken into account.

2. Vision creates conflict that must be managed and balanced between the demands of the present and the expectations and forces of the future.

3. Communication of the vision must be ongoing.

   A vision that is not understood remains a mere occurrence; understood, it becomes a living experience.—Carl Jung

4. Recruit very carefully, for potential employees display their assets and mask their defects. There must be total honesty on the part of the employer concerning company work ethics, behaviors, and attitudes. Communication begins at the top.

5. Provide incentives and rewards for employees for the achievement of the purpose and the vision.

6. Provide for the ongoing evaluation of your progress (and your self-development).

   Measurements are a tool for making things better; not a performance hammer.—H. Darrell Young

7. Expand educational programs for employees.

8. Organize to meet customer needs.

9. Communicating the vision is about being right, but more than being right, communicating is about understanding, trust, and support.

10. In the final analysis, to manage the vision, we must:

    - Live the vision where others see it in us.
    - Let others know how they are contributing.
    - Make a commitment to learn, unlearn, and relearn.
    - Serve people and never forget their value.
    - Never get overly discouraged.

How It Fits: The Relationship of Values, Beliefs, Purpose, Vision, Mission, Strategies, and Measurements

There seems to be one question left that all leaders need to answer: "How do I get from my beliefs, my purpose, my vision, and my mission to bring *uniformity* to the workplace, organization, team, or group, etc.?" Another way of asking this question is "How do I get others to buy into my vision?" If you have already asked yourself this question, then you have taken the first step in answering it. Many who are in positions of leadership never ask themselves this question and, quite frankly, usually experience disharmony and disloyalty among those who are in the organization.

Examining the graphic on the next page, we discover that the *key* is how to move from personal beliefs and values to group or organizational beliefs and values. There are two issues here:

- The current knowledge you have of your vision. There is no substitute for clarity of belief, purpose, mission, or vision. Effective leaders understand this fact. Therefore, the first commandment of leadership is "Know Thyself." This does not mean that leaders can't change, be flexible, or compromise. It does mean that seldom will leaders change their core values or beliefs. Leadership begins with belief—in self and in others. To unify the workforce or organization, there are many areas where we can change and other places where we can reach compromises. Seldom will we give up our core beliefs. For example, a principal of a school may negotiate class size, time and schedules, and even methodologies with teachers and supervisors, but the principal will never negotiate his or her belief that every child can learn and deserves the best education he or she is able to provide.

- Your understanding of how to sell your vision to others in your organization and move them to action. Does this mean compromise? Yes it does. Does it mean giving up one's core beliefs? No it does not. Just like the superintendent of a school system, principals, teachers, and central office supervisors are also leaders. They too have fundamental beliefs, values, and visions—for themselves and for those around them. The mark of leadership is the ability to bring unity to the greater organization without requiring total uniformity from every person who works in the organization. What is important here is *finding agreement on those core beliefs* that define the mission of the organization and, at the same time, allows others within the system to pursue personal, departmental, or group visions.

EXAMPLE:

Jack is a teacher at River Bend Middle School. Through meetings with his principal and central office middle school supervisor, the core beliefs of the school system have been outlined; namely, (1) that every child can learn, (2) that middle school age children have certain needs different from elementary and high school students, and (3) that there is no substitute for excellence in teaching. After examining his own beliefs about education—teaching and learning—Jack agrees that these three beliefs are fundamental to his work and to the work of every teacher, principal, supervisor, and superintendent within his school system.

But Jack tells his principal that he has some other goals that he wants to pursue and he believes that these are consistent with the vision, mission, and beliefs of the school system. Jack wants to return to school during the summer months and pursue the masters and doctorate degrees in education. He says that he ultimately would like to teach in a college situation. His principal tells him that he should pursue these advanced degrees, but while doing it, use the information that he is learning to improve his classroom methods. Jack is relieved that his principal is not threatened by his desire to return to college and agrees that it will help improve him personally and the school where he is teaching.

Leaders need to understand that unity can be achieved without total uniformity and that the effectiveness of the organization depends on the continuous value improvement of each member, which also means personal growth and development. Leaders need to understand that they do indeed set a directional focus through their vision; that the needs of workers and consumers are always changing, which requires continuous evaluation and flexibility on his or her part; and that leadership effectiveness entails energizing workers and creating an environment where leadership can emerge at all levels.

Know Thyself—First Commandment of Leadership

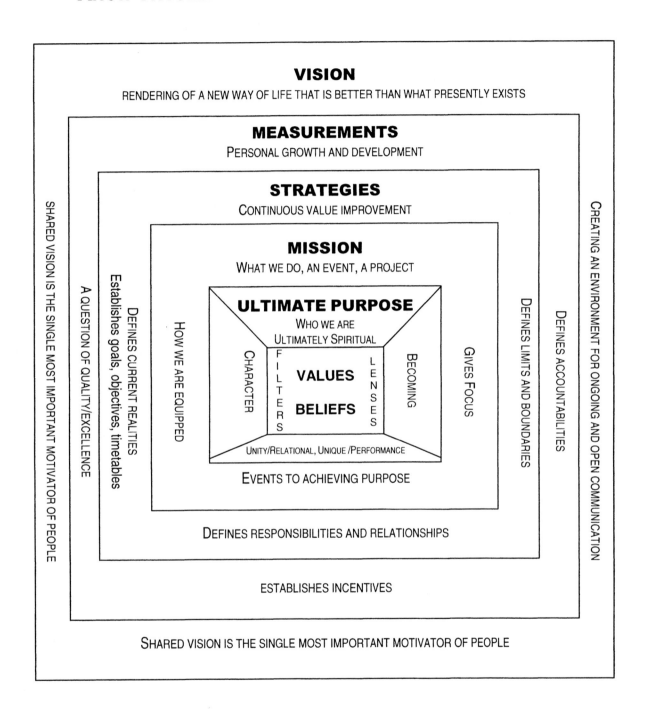

VISION
RENDERING OF A NEW WAY OF LIFE THAT IS BETTER THAN WHAT PRESENTLY EXISTS

MEASUREMENTS
PERSONAL GROWTH AND DEVELOPMENT

STRATEGIES
CONTINUOUS VALUE IMPROVEMENT

MISSION
WHAT WE DO, AN EVENT, A PROJECT

ULTIMATE PURPOSE
WHO WE ARE
ULTIMATELY SPIRITUAL

CHARACTER

FILTERS

VALUES

BELIEFS

LENSES

BECOMING

UNITY/RELATIONAL, UNIQUE /PERFORMANCE

EVENTS TO ACHIEVING PURPOSE

GIVES FOCUS

HOW WE ARE EQUIPPED

DEFINES CURRENT REALITIES
Establishes goals, objectives, timetables

A QUESTION OF QUALITY/EXCELLENCE

SHARED VISION IS THE SINGLE MOST IMPORTANT MOTIVATOR OF PEOPLE

DEFINES LIMITS AND BOUNDARIES

DEFINES ACCOUNTABILITIES

CREATING AN ENVIRONMENT FOR ONGOING AND OPEN COMMUNICATION

DEFINES RESPONSIBILITIES AND RELATIONSHIPS

ESTABLISHES INCENTIVES

SHARED VISION IS THE SINGLE MOST IMPORTANT MOTIVATOR OF PEOPLE

A PERSONAL BUSINESS PLAN

PART 2
CONTINUOUS IMPROVEMENT

Transformance Not Promises

Transformance Not Promises is about leadership transformation through ongoing learning and development and leadership performance that is characterized by behavior and discipline. The first thing we must do is to improve ourselves; improving others will follow our leadership.

PART 2 EMPHASIZES THREE FUNDAMENTAL CONCEPTS:

Why Transformation Is Not an Option

Transformation Strategies

Quality As the Performance Measure

TRANSFORMANCE NOT PROMISES ▶

Linking Purpose with Performance

Concepts for Building a Leadership Culture

Part 2 of *Leadership under Construction* serves as a bridge between building a leadership foundation (part 1) and building a leadership culture (part 3). The objective of part 2 is to achieve agreement on the basic principle that "leadership development is a commitment to self-development and is achieved through lifelong learning, thinking, and consistent ethical living." Part 1 focused on creating a plan and a standard for leadership development. Part 3 focuses on the importance of relationships and how networking influences the development of ideas, methods, and leadership success.

Part 2 challenges us to take an inside look at ourselves, especially our choice and commitment to become a leader. Make no mistake about it, leadership development is not easy; it requires continuous learning, growth, and personal improvement. It also means embracing unnatural behaviors and disciplines and learning to embrace change as a dynamic force of improvement.

Here we learn that leaders are faced with significant internal and external changes that will sometime result in obstacles and roadblocks. These difficulties have the potential of preventing leaders from achieving their goal of continuous transformation and quality performance. This material will challenge the student of leadership to recognize, evaluate, and make a positive decision for personal transformation. It will challenge them to take actions against many of these forces, some of which were imposed on them and over which they have little control.

Making either positive or negative change in one's character and behavior are actions that touch the organizational community like ripples in a pond. They often collide against old habits and traditions, challenging our ability to communicate and influence others, and challenging our internal messenger who is telling us to be careful and go slowly. Students of leadership must be encouraged to accept the realities of their world as opportunities for significant change. Our premise is that many of the circumstances that seem to block us in our daily lives may only appear to do so based on a framework of assumptions we carry with us. Draw a different frame around the same set of circumstances and new pathways come into view. Find the right framework and extraordinary accomplishment becomes an everyday experience. We are challenged to take advantage of the uncertainty, unpredictability, and volatility that has become a way of life for the 21st century.

This section provides suggestions for novel ways of defining others, the world in which we live, and ourselves. It is about rearranging, creating surprising juxtapositions, emotional openings, and startling presences. This book offers practices that are transformational—that may feel illogical or counterintuitive to our normal understanding of how things operate. Their purpose is to initiate a new approach to current conditions, based on uncommon assumptions about the nature of the world.

The forces of change for the 21st century are many: technology, demographic movements, cultural clashes, economic ups and downs, and family differences. Alone, we are hopeless as we try to manipulate through the changes brought on by these forces. Our future depends on our willingness to continually reevaluate and reshape what, how, why, where, and when we address our current environments. Accepting the realities of these changes is the first step in controlling their impact on our lives. We can try to control these forces or be controlled by them; in the end, it is a matter of choosing how we respond to the question: "Can I really change?" or "Can we really change?"

Another premise that underlies leadership transformation is that transformation is not really an option. Leaders either initiate change and transformation in themselves and their organizations or are changed by the internal and external forces of their working environments. Ancient wisdom tells us, you can't put new wine into old wineskins. The new wine will burst the old skins, spilling the wine and ruining the skins. This idea should perhaps be discussed in class where students are allowed to examine examples that illustrate its timeless truth.

As leaders or potential leaders we have been given the responsibility of creating a future of our own choosing. This choice and how we exercise it will determine our future. Success will follow if we remain flexible, reflect rather than merely respond to incoming stimuli, and act wisely. After all, life is an invention. Once you have begun to distinguish that *it's all invented,* you can create a place to live and work where new inventions are the order of the day—a place called "the universe of possibility."

Part 2 will help you deal with these issues, especially the issue of choosing to lead and take the initiative to transform yourself. Leadership is a result of self-invention and self-reinvention. It is a continuous process of self-appraisal and dealing with change. Inventing oneself, giving birth to oneself, is not the same as accepting the roles we were brought up to play. In the universe of possibility, you set the context and let life unfold; you are not at the mercy of outside or inside pressures. Thus, we must remember, our lives are founded on a network of hidden assumptions. If we learn to notice and distinguish these assumptions, we will be able to break through the barriers of any "box" that contains unwanted conditions and create other conditions that support the life we envision for our self and those around us. Self-invention is dynamic and creative. It starts with the internal focus of self-reflection and becomes a process of personal transformation.

Part 2 is the bridge between parts 1 and 3. Part 1 helps leaders determine their destination; part 2 helps them access their personal value; and part 3 helps them determine who will step up and become a leader and who will choose to continually grow as a leader. Review and think through the following quotes in preparation for teaching this material:

FACT

We live in a moment in time where the rate of change is so speeded up, we see the future only as it is disappearing.—R. D. Laing

REALITY

Most of us can see the handwriting on the wall; we just think it's addressed to someone else.—Unknown

Faced with having to change our views, or prove there is no reason not to, most of us get busy on the proving.—John Kenneth Galbraith

OPPORTUNITY

This time like all others is a good one if we but know what to do with it.—Ralph Waldo Emerson

Ethical Leadership for Public School Administrators and Teachers

A new book written by Dr. Joseph P. Hester and published by McFarland & Company, Inc., focuses on "leading from the inside out," from one's character. In the first workbook, students were asked to read the first three chapters of that book and utilize some of the exercises at the end of the chapters. The book can be used as a self-contained workbook; each chapter has exercises that engage the minds of participants. Here, we are using some of these exercises in conjunction with *Leadership under Construction.* This will give added depth and meaning to this course of study. Before proceeding with the exercises in this workbook, ask students to read chapter 4 of *Ethical Leadership.* Have students complete the exercises (1–8) and discuss their answers thoroughly.

ICE-BREAKERS

One method of breaking down barriers and warming the class to discussion and dialogue is to have them respond to significant quotes. Use your judgment about when and where to use these quotes, but do use them for they bring significant attention to the principles and concepts of leadership.

If there is no transformation inside each of us, all the structural change in the world will have no impact on our institutions.—Peter Block

We have no choice but to invite people into the process of rethinking, redesigning, restructuring the organization. We ignore people's need to participate at our own peril.—Margaret Wheatley

Within every organization, there is a cluster of interconnected communities of practice. The more people are engaged in these informal networks, and the more developed and sophisticated the networks are, the better will the organization be able to learn, respond creatively to unexpected new circumstances, change, and evolve. In other words, the organization's aliveness resides in its communities of practice.—Fritjof Capra, *The Hidden Connections*

Transformation Is Not an Option

CONCEPT 2.1

We are in transition from an old to a new system that is driven by interconnected forces of change that require personal transformation.

Most of us can see the handwriting on the wall; we just think it's addressed to someone else.—Unknown

Purpose:

The purpose of this section is to understand that the world is changing and that transforming ourselves to meet changing situations is a necessity, not an option. Our intellectual capabilities and those with whom we work are our greatest assets.

Procedures:

- Be sure to have them read chapter 4 of *Helping Educators Lead*. The exercises at the end of chapter 4 provide a springboard to understanding the concepts in this workbook.

- The *Icebreakers* will engage students' minds and help them focus on transformation and continuous self-improvement.

Activities:

- Review the page "Environmental Realities of the 21st Century." Have students complete activity 17, "Managing Change."

- Continue by discussing "Two Interconnected Forces of Change" and engage students in activities 18 and 19.

ENVIRONMENTAL REALITIES OF THE 21ST CENTURY

Today the formalities are gone and change is upon us like a whirlwind. While whirlwinds may have a clear direction from a distance, it is a vastly different thing to be caught in one. There is no way to see its direction, understand how the various pieces come together, or comprehend its force. You simply get caught up and thrown around.—Michael Annison, *Managing the Whirlwind*

What we learn from Annison are the following about "change" and "environmental change":

1. The speed of change is accelerating:

    *   Uncertainty, turbulence, and unpredictability—major forces of change—have resulted in increased complexity, volatility, and ambiguity. Offshore outsourcing and changes in technology, demographics, values, and the persistent pressures of globalization are sustaining this condition.

    *   Change has become a way of life, the norm, not the exception.

2. The changes we are experiencing are pervasive:

    *   They can be compared to one thousand rocks dropped simultaneously in a pond. The metaphor is clear: the ripples and vibrations of these changes touch us all as they overlap and collide in our daily lives.

    *   Yesterday was sympathetic to our desire for predictability, introducing the puzzle of change—piece by piece—allowing us to digest and assimilate these pieces in some quantity before we had to act on them or continue to the next changing situation.

3. These changes require that we redefine and reengineer how our world works as well as develop a new understanding of the value of an individual in that new world.

    *   Therefore, we are required to reevaluate and reshape what we do, how we do it and why we do it, where we do it and when we do it. Modification is not enough!

    *   These changes force us to rewrite the rules and shift basic assumptions in order to solve problems more efficiently.

The single greatest challenge facing managers in the developed countries of the world is to raise the productivity of knowledge and service workers.—Peter Drucker

TO THE TEACHER

The following topics or concept connections have been very effective with students, especially college age and adults. Before engaging students in activity 17, use these to stimulate their minds and clarify their thoughts about *managing change:*

1. Short-term versus long-term thinking (Instant gratification versus vision)

2. Balance of behaviors and disciplines (Leading up and managing down)

3. Internal value creation versus acquisition (Creating future value versus acquiring market share)

4. Revenue generation versus expense control (Business model sustainability)

5. Role of customers and employees (Revenue growth and profit)

6. One time payment versus ongoing cost (The cost of a leadership culture)

7. Globalization, character, and culture (Right versus wrong issues)

The teacher needs to use personal judgment regarding the choice of these topics, making sure they fit the audience and continue the discussion about leadership and change.

Activity 17: Managing Change

Directions: The activity below is a continuation of the work begun in the first book (part 1) of this leadership-training program. Complete each section in as much detail as you are able to provide.

1. In part 1 of this training you developed a vision, purpose, and mission for your organization. Take time now to review those statements and write a summary of them below:

_____

_____

_____

_____

_____

_____

2. In the space below, describe *how* changes in the marketplace are today—and perhaps will be in the future—affecting your organization (business, school, church, etc.):

_____

_____

_____

_____

_____

_____

3. In the space below, describe the possible responses (changes) your organization must make to meet the challenges and opportunities of this changing marketplace:

_____

_____

_____

_____

_____

_____

_____

_____

4. Finally, describe _how_ the value of you and others have changed in the past decade and how your organization is responding to this "new-found" value:

_____

_____

_____

_____

_____

_____

_____

_____

TWO INTERCONNECTED FORCES OF CHANGE

Two of the driving forces responsible for the accelerated, pervasive, redefining changes of our contemporary environment are the following:

- The transition from an industrial age to an information/technological age, to a service age.

- A challenge to balance leadership capacities and management skills

Consider the following:

1. The Information Age has brought us many new and exciting challenges. It requires a total reevaluation of how we fit, behaviorally, intellectually, interpersonally, and spiritually into this environment. The Information Age is today defined as the age of the *thinker/problem-solver* who understands the value of linking thought with purpose. As we think our way through this evolving age we are learning that information can become knowledge, yet this new knowledge is of no real value apart from the service of others and ourselves. Therefore, our information/knowledge age will become an age of service.

2. How important does that make the development of interpersonal skills for future success? As a result of the continued increase of information, businesses, schools, and organizations are becoming, to a large part, collections of specialists. The greater our commitment to knowledge and education, the more specialized resources become and the more specialized our resources, the further away we are from those we serve.

3. The further we move from the ones we intend to serve the more dependent we become on each other's specialization. Interestingly, there is built into the Information/Service Age a requirement of interdependence—a dependence on the expertise of each other for continued success and sustainability.

4. Leaders have additional duties. Not only are they required to be excellent specialists, but they are also called upon to play the role of generalist and take conceptual leaps across disciplines and make connections that specialists sometimes can't see. This is the age of information, knowledge, and service.

In this section, these transitions or paradigm shifts will be discussed with an emphasis on the vision, character (beliefs, values, and purposes), and attitude adjustments that must be made in order to balance the new behaviors and the old disciplines with the leadership requirements of the 21st century. Teachers should understand that there are many other interconnected forces of change that will come up in the discussion. Among these are technology, globalization, demographics, and the debate about value relativity that is often found in the emphasis on multiculturalism. The interconnected forces of change require some unnatural behaviors such as (1) embracing newness, (2) letting go of the past, (3) finding joy in adversity, and (4) enhanced discipline.

Transition from an Industrial Age to an Information/Technological Age, to a Service Age—Paradigm Shifts (model, pattern, ways of doing things)

A paradigm is a model or view of the world that shapes our understanding, our view of things. This can be individual or cultural, Peter Drucker says, "Each of us behaves in accordance with a theory or paradigm whether we are aware of it or not. Each person develops his/her own paradigm through personal life experiences; therefore, each person views the world differently and responds differently in certain situations. During a paradigm shift, we must challenge the deeply ingrained assumptions and problem solving strategies that make up our view of the world, as well as gaining agreement with others on a new set of rules that is in sync with the requirement of the shift."

Speaking about the reform movement in public schooling, Phillip C. Schlechty noted in 1990 that much of this movement has grown from a concern that schools are not preparing students "to compete in the emerging information-based global economy." The concept of "information-based global economy" represents a paradigm shift in the way we think about schools as well as businesses. Schlechty says, "Such a redesign must begin . . . with a fundamental reconceptualization of the purpose and vision that will provide the framework out of which restructured schools might emerge to meet the needs of the twenty-first century."

As expected, Schlechty finds his new model in Peter Drucker's emphasis on *information-based, knowledge-based, knowledge work,* and *learning-based,* all of which describe the new era in which we now live. He defines "knowledge work" as "putting to use ideas and symbols to produce some purposeful result . . . thus, the term 'knowledge work' focuses attention on the idea of expending mental effort." He includes in this paradigm service-oriented work and says, "America is becoming an information-based, service-oriented society. . . . The point is that the basis for manufacturing will shift from an emphasis on machinery and muscle to an emphasis on the management and use of knowledge." See: *Schools for the 21st Century, Leadership Imperatives for Education Reform,* 1990, 34ff.

THE INDUSTRIAL AGE: DEFINING CHARACTERISTICS

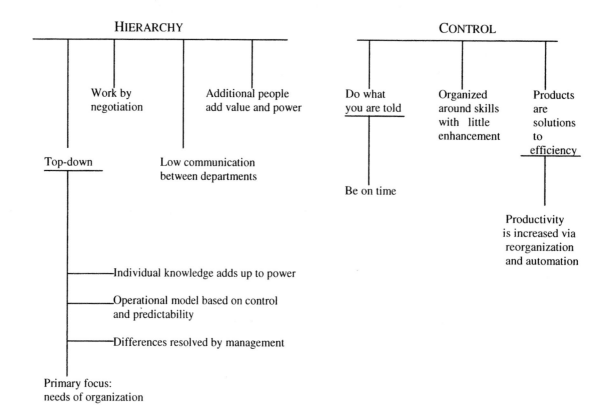

This chart can be used as an example as is or you can substitute "parents" or "old boss" of any former job. Discuss with students what they have experienced as negative examples of leadership that fit this model before moving forward.

THE INFORMATION AGE: DEFINING CHARACTERISTICS AND CONNECTIONS

Reevaluating Paradigms	A Portfolio of Skills Focusing on Information Workers	Information: Cultural and Organizational Shifts
• Competition and survival to collaboration and cooperation.	• Knowledge is the primary asset.	• Free communications, regardless of rank and power.
• Feeling of having learned it all to learning never stops.	• Knowledge workers have decision-making power.	• Influence based on competence and knowledge, rather than power and agenda.
• Carry out policy to individual problem solving.	• Knowledge workers are responsible for their own continuous learning.	• Conflict resolution based on consensus, rather than coercion.
• People are expendable to people are the greatest asset.	• Knowledge workers are responsible for the standards of their own work.	• Mediating cultural diversity by rational means.
• Organizational hierarchy to networking.	• Knowledge workers improve and grow based on self-imposed demands.	• Encouraging professional growth.
• Market share to market creation.	• Knowledge workers are major investment/costs centers.	• Creating an innovative reward system.
• Title and rank to making a difference.	• Knowledge workers have no superiors or subordinates.	• Adapting to temporary work/relationship situations.
• Quality-affordable best to quality with no compromise.	• Knowledge workers are the tools of production.	• Ongoing reinvention of leadership.
• Motivation to complete to motivation to build.	• Knowledge workers define work as a collection of projects that meet consumer needs.	• Challenging traditional values/ways of completing tasks, and conventional wisdom.
• Risk-adverse culture to risk-prone culture.		• Accepting uncertainty as a strength.
• Self-fulfillment to service fulfillment.	• Knowledge workers focus on functions rather than on departments and how they are structured.	• Becoming more creative, innovative, and adaptive.
• Short-term goals to long-term goals.		
See: Warren Bennis	• Knowledge workers maximize opportunity by changing faster than the environment itself.	Drucker, Peter F. *The Effective Executive.* New York: Harper and Row, 1966.

You Can't Change Behavior
Until You Change the Focus

▸ Focus on the needs of the organization. ▸ Gets its work done through people.	▸ Focus on the needs of the people. ▸ Service is the lifestyle of the organization.
INDUSTRIAL AGE	**INFORMATION AGE**

SERVING

Directors	Consumers
CEOs	Employees
VPs	Supervisors
Superintendents	Managers
Principals	Principals
Managers	Superintendents
Supervisors	VPs
Employees	CEOs
Consumers	Directors

*All organizations are service organizations to the degree
that they create consumer value through performance.*

The Orchestra

Peter Drucker (Jack Beatty, *The World According to Peter Drucker*, 1998) has talked about the idea of an orchestra being the model for an organization. In an orchestra, every member "knows the score." Each person knows the total piece they are playing as well as their own part. Orchestras have no hierarchies; everybody works. The first violinist plays, as well as managing, coordinating, and working with the rest of the violinists. An orchestra always practices. Some of these practices are public performances, but the focus is on continually getting better. An orchestra is highly interdependent; the whole depends on each person knowing the score and doing his or her part. Mistakes reflect on the entire orchestra. Finally, the leadership of the orchestra—the conductor—can rarely play any of the instruments he or she conducts. The responsibility of the leadership is to focus on the overall purpose of the orchestra, and to help each member accomplish what needs to be done.

Democracy becomes a functional necessity whenever a social system is competing for survival under conditions of chronic change.—Warren Bennis, *Teaching Old Dogs New Tricks*, 1999

Activity 18: Leadership Style Evaluation

1. Evaluate the current leadership/management style of your organization. Is your current style more like the industrial age top-down style or more like the information age bottom-up style? Write your answer in the space below and justify your response with specific examples and behaviors that you have observed:

_____

_____

_____

_____

_____

_____

_____

2. Carefully review the current leadership/mangement style you have described above for your organization. Make any corrections or additions that need to be made. In the space below, prioritize three to five steps you believe are needed to change your organization's style for the better:

_____

_____

_____

_____

_____

_____

_____

_____

Activity 19: Describing Your Organization

Directions: Read the story "The Orchestra," and note how Peter Drucker explains the idea of an organization using an orchestra as a positive model or metaphor for how an organization should work in our knowledge, service-oriented world. Complete the activities in the spaces provided below:

1. What metaphor best describes your organization? Write a description below using as many details as possible to flesh out the style, commitments, and values of your organization:

_____

_____

_____

_____

_____

_____

_____

_____

_____

_____

_____

_____

_____

_____

2. Compare and contrast your organization with that of "The Orchestra." How are they alike and how are they different? What patterns emerge from your comparisons require changing? What patterns emerge that need further support and widespread articulation?

YOUR ORGANIZATION	THE ORCHESTRA

Patterns that need revising or more support:

3. In the list of paradigms provided in the three columns under the heading "The Information Age: Defining Characteristics," which in each set best describes your organization? Refer to activity 16 to help with this exercise. List these and justify your responses:

LIST OF BEHAVIORS	JUSTIFIED RESPONSES

CONCEPT 2.2

Intellectual capital has become the greatest asset of the 21st century and will require the behavior of a leader balanced with the discipline of a manager.

Purpose:

- The purpose of this section is to understand the challenges of balancing leadership and management capabilities and skills.

Procedure:

- Share concept 2.2 with students and then discuss the differences between a leader and a manager.

Activities:

- Share the differences between managers and leaders with the class and then complete activity 20.

- Conclude with a discussion of "Leading and Managing" and complete activity 21.

- Summarize this section with a discussion of "Things to Remember."

The Challenge to Balance Leadership and Management Capabilities and Skills

Management and Leadership Differences

MANAGEMENT	LEADERSHIP
Latin root: "to hand" (implies handling things)	Latin root: "to go" (implies moving forward)
Something you do	Something you are
Efficiency	Effectiveness
"How"	"What" and "Why"
A science	An art
Gets people to do	Gets people to want to do
Deals with efficient use of resources such as time, material, money, and manpower	Deals with motivation and unification of people toward a common cause or purpose.
Comes from a position of power	Comes from a position of influence
Focuses on actions	Focuses on attitudes and behavior
Promotes stability	Presses for change
Plans, organizes, staffs organization for orderly results	Strategies, patterns, relationships, alignment, and communication create value
Sign language: holding on to, like you would the reigns of a horse or restraining something	Sign language: cradling of your arms and rocking back and forth the way a parent would nurture a child

Activity 20: Evaluating Where You Fit

Directions: Evaluate yourself by marking either **M** or **L** in each blank: **SCORE: M___ L___**

MANAGERS	M/I	LEADERS
Administer, Imitate, Maintain ▶ Perpetuates existing establishment ▶ Concentrates on strategies, analysis ▶ Conserves assets ▶ Wants good work—"If not broken, don't fix it!"		**Innovate, Originate, Develop** ▶ Encourages vision and imagination ▶ Nurtures cultures, values sharing ▶ Risk assets ▶ Demands better work
Focus on Structure ▶ Process, predictability, and systems ▶ Management levels and hierarchy ▶ Trusts process, limits risks ▶ Thinks rivals ▶ Controls people		**Focus on People** ▶ Overcomes process by creative action ▶ Flat organizations ▶ Trusts people; accepts failure ▶ Thinks partners ▶ Empowers people
Rely on Control ▶ How decisions are made ▶ Communicates to a few experts ▶ Uses authority ▶ Seeks uniformity		**Inspire Trust** ▶ What decisions are made ▶ Communicates to all the people ▶ Uses influences ▶ Seeks unity
Have Short-term View ▶ Eyes on bottom line ▶ Serves markets ▶ Mind on present		**Have Long-term Perspective** ▶ Eyes on horizon ▶ Serve customers ▶ Mind on the future
Accepts Status Quo ▶ Avoids direct confrontation that stirs opposition ▶ MBO (Manages by Objectives) ▶ Yearns for stability ▶ Trained: answers, closed common sense, rigid		**Challenges Status Quo** ▶ Turns problems into opportunities ▶ MBWA (Manages by Walking Around) ▶ Thrive on crisis ▶ Educated: questions, open, imagination, flexible
A Copy: Changes with Political Climate ▶ Style ▶ Air of superiority ▶ Have few convictions with passion ▶ High degree of fair-mindedness		**An Original: Their Own Person** ▶ Substance ▶ Attitude ▶ Strong convictions ▶ High level of ethics and values

Majority of content based on Warren Bennis, HBO Conference, 1990

LEADING AND MANAGING

We are a nation that has been over-managed and under-led. We lost our leadership when we moved to managing things rather than leading people.—Grace Hooper, From a speech given at HBO

Can an Individual Lead and Manage Effectively?

We should remember:

• Managers are necessary, but leaders are essential.

• Management is of the mind, but leadership is of the heart.

• A key to success in the 21st century is to determine
  when to manage, when to lead, under what circumstances,
  and for how long.

As Peter Drucker suggests, in the information-based organization, the concept of span of control—the ideas that a manager can effectively manage no more than seven plus-or-minus subordinates—is replaced with the concept of span of communication. In a network organization, it is the kinds of communications and the relationship among teams and team members working together to solve problems that must be "managed." The key to adding value, to turning knowledge into a distinctive competence, involves the flexible development of a multitude of relationships.—Paul Leinberger and Bruce Tucker

Activity 21: Leading and Managing

Directions: Now that you have evaluated yourself using activity 18, think about the various organizations of which you are or have been a part. Pick one of these (school, team, club, church, classroom, business, etc.) and complete the following activity: in the *left-hand column* list the characteriestics that define the leadership and management of your chosen organization, and in the *right-hand column,* list any leadership and management skills that are needed to make this organization more responsive to its purpose and more efficient in its actions.

There will probably be big differences in perception and/or reality between the student and the organization. Discussing these differences will be essential to participant understanding.

CHARACTERISTICS THAT DEFINE YOUR ORGANIZATION	SKILLS NEEDED FOR ORGANIZATIONAL IMPROVEMENT

THE 21ST CENTURY REQUIREMENTS

THE BEHAVIOR OF A LEADER (SERVANT) BALANCED BY
THE DISCIPLINE OF A MANAGER (STEWARD)

The words "manager" and "leader" are metaphors representing two opposite ends of the continuum. For example: Tom Landry is a consummate manager, while John Madden is a committed leader. In effective leaders, leadership and management skills are balanced and coordinated. In periods of accelerated change there will always be a need to manage existing operations and keep them under control, while at the same time leading the organization into new avenues that are flexible, creative, and innovative. Timing and balance are the issues

We need to integrate all the principles of management and leadership, blending both innovation and stability, both order and flexibility.—Peter Drucker

The purpose of this section is to show what happens when a balance has not been achieved between leading and managing. Fundamentally, management involves strategic, short-term planning and leading involves vision and long-term frameworks. Ideally, an effective leader must possess both leadership and management skills.

Over-emphasis on management will bring to the organization the following:

- Emphasis on short time frames

- Emphasis on details, short-term planning, and budgeting

- Elimination of risk-taking behaviors and innovation

- Emphasis on scientific management principles

- Focus on rule compliance and structure

- Focus on fitting people to jobs

- Focus on control and predictability

Over-emphasis on leadership will bring to the organization the following:

- Strong long-term vision; the big picture, but may lack focus on today's execution

- Innovation, but may not maximize product/services life cycles

- Value of people, but may not balance personal growth with performance measurements

- Alignment of vision with practice, but may neglect rewards

- Empowerment, but may abdicate responsibilities

IDEALLY, MANAGEMENT AND LEADERSHIP MUST BE KEPT IN BALANCE!

THINGS TO REMEMBER

- We are in transition from an old to a new system that is driven by interconnected forces of accelerating change.

- Built into the Information Age is the requirement to depend on each other.

- During periods of extreme transition, strength will be discovered not in our quest for stability and sameness, but in our ability to adapt and make change the nature of ourselves.

- Adaptability has become the most important determinant of organizational survival as it drives the organization of the future.

- The only thing an organization in the Information Age has that appreciates in value is the capability of its people.

- As we move into the 21st century, we seem to have an abundance of managers, but a shortage of leaders, and almost no integration of the two.

- Neglect of service is indicative of an organization that is becoming more self-centered; an organization that requires being served and gives more attention to getting than giving.

- People manage, people lead, and people always do both imperfectly.

CONTROLLING CHANGE

OR CONTROLLED BY CHANGE

CONCEPT 2.3

There is an increasing gap between the behaviors and attitudes that were responsible for our past successes and the behaviors and attitudes that will be responsible for our successes in the future.

Purpose:

- Continue the discussion of change and transformation with concept 2.3 and the section that follows concept 2.3: "For Your Consideration."

Procedures:

- Use "Things to Remember" from the previous section to aid the discussion of change and transformation.

- On the following pages, cover "Challenges and Consequences of Successful Leadership" to focus on purposeful change.

- Finally, share "The Problem: Understanding and Overcoming Obstacles and Challenges of Resisting Change and Resisting Being Changed." Discuss with class and ask for personal examples.

Activities:

- Complete activity 22 and bring section to a close with a discussion of the "Four Requirements for Managing Change" and "Things to Remember."

For Your Consideration:

Before there were rocket launching technologies that propelled nets over trees to capture monkeys for our zoos, man devised a very simple method for capturing monkeys that I believe is relative to how many of us deal with changing times. The first step to capture was to find a coconut and cut a small hole in its top and pour out the juice. Second, the capturer would extract as much of the fruit as possible and place beans that the monkeys considered a delicacy in the bottom of the coconut. Third, the capturer would nail the coconut to a tree. During the day Mr. or Mrs. Monkey (depending on our preference) would come along and smell the beans in the coconut. With an opened hand, the monkey would reach into the coconut and grab a fistfull of beans. You can begin to see the problem. The monkey had no difficulty getting his/her opened hand into the coconut; however, he or she could not get a closed fist out of the coconut. Herein lies the problem: Would the monkey let go of the beans and not risk capture but loose a delicious meal, or would the monkey keep the beans and eventually be captured? You guessed it! CAPTURED!! The question for us is:

WILL I LET GO OF THE PAST—*THE BEANS*—

IN ORDER TO PRESERVE MY PRESENT AND FUTURE FREEDOM?

CHALLENGES AND CONSEQUENCES OF
SUCCESSFUL LEADERSHIP

CHALLENGES OF THE GAP	CONSEQUENCES OF THE GAP
• Never have we faced so many challenges and so many choices with which to face those challenges.	• Organization restructures to enhance productivity
• Balancing the need to learn from the past and simultaneously design the future.	• Consolidation of functions
• Getting people to unlearn behaviors that have made them successful in the past and will cause them to fail in the future.	• Elimination of levels
	• Forced reinvention of employees
• Learning to control changing events rather than being controlled by them	• Frustrated and fearful employees
	• Transference of loyalty to skills rather than companies and people

There is nothing more difficult to carry out nor more doubtful of success nor more dangerous to handle than to initiate a new order of things.—Machiavelli

This time like all others is a good one if we but know what to do with it.—Ralph Waldo Emerson

Change is the measure of our time; how we handle it is the measure of ourselves.—Joe Hester

THE PROBLEM

UNDERSTANDING AND OVERCOMING OBSTACLES AND CHALLENGES OF RESISTING CHANGE AND RESISTING BEING CHANGED

In one year 98 percent of all the atoms making up our bodies are exchanged for new ones; therefore, within one year we become new people—physically. Our lives are an endless flow of change. So what is the problem with change?

We continually and persistently resist change!

Reasons We Resist Change

- Uninformed judgments and lack of imagination

- Lack of understanding of methods or procedures (approaches to change)

- Embarrassment as a result of the unknown

- Uncertainty, doubt, and a desire for stability

- Too much risk

- Change means additional trouble and work, and we are preoccupied with the present

- Change starts with the person in the mirror and brings new responsibilities and accountabilities.

- Change forces us to unhook biases, prejudices, and traditions, and to forget past successes and failures.

- Changing our behavior is costly

- Change requires giving up control

Faced with having to change our views or prove there is no need to, most of us get busy on the proving.—John Kenneth Galbraith

Activity 22: ALMOST ALL CHANGE UPSETS THE COMFORT OF OUR MINDS

Directions: This activity is based on the concept of "Think-Pair-Share." Students will be divided into pairs (if there is an odd number, one pair can become a threesome). Each person in the pair will list three to five reasons he/she tends to resist change. Once this has been completed, each will share his/her reasons. Give five minutes for writing and allow students six or seven minutes to share their responses. Finally, working together, each pair will make a list of *how* they think they can overcome their resistance to change. These will then be shared with the entire class.

REASONS "I" CAN RESIST	HOW "WE" CAN OVERCOME OUR RESISTANCE TO CHANGE

MANAGING CHANGE FOR A LIFETIME

Many leaders are cut short because they won't adjust their behaviors, styles, or methods to changing situations. Charles Spurgeon, one of the great preachers of the 20th century, says that he was shrewd enough to see the need for changing his methods and style of ministry but neither flexible nor versatile enough to make the changes that the times demanded. As a result, his effectiveness with second-generation congregations suffered.

FOUR REQUIREMENTS FOR MANAGING CHANGE

1. Embracing two realities

- The future will be different from the past

- The present is not our final and highest achievement

2. Insight without commitment leads to frustration

- Insight of the type of change (revolution, reformation, or innovation)

- Insight of acceptable implementation of criteria (an easier way, ease of transition, small wins, flexibility, a better way)

3. Timing is as important as event

- The timing of circumstances

- The timing of communication

- The timing of action, what, and when:

  - The wrong action at the wrong time leads to disaster

  - The right action at the wrong time brings resistance

  - The wrong action at the right time is a mistake

  - The right action at the right time results in success

4. Change can be destructive

- When we don't know and are uncertain about the facts

- When the burden of change leads to crisis

- When the concern about doing things right (efficiency) supersedes doing the right things (effectiveness)

BUT CAN WE REALLY CHANGE?

▶ We have been given the responsibility to create a future of our own choosing. This responsibility of choice and how we exercise it will determine our actions as we pursue that future.

▶ We will not be able to effectively deal with the accelerated, pervasive forces of change unless we have stability of who we are and what we are striving to become.

▶ Real change requires stability, flexibility, discipline, and balance.

THINGS TO REMEMBER

•   Behaviors and attitudes that were responsible for our past successes may cause us to fail in the future..

•   Our ability to learn, unlearn, and relearn is a key sustainable competitive advantage in the 21st century.

•   Change is a measure of our times, how we handle it is a measure of ourselves.

•   The future will be different from the past and the present is not our final and highest achievement.

•   People resist change and being changed. We always believe the old is better.

The single greatest challenge facing managers in the developed countries of the world is to raise the productivity of knowledge and service workers. This challenge will ultimately determine the competitive performance of companies. Even more important, it will determine the very fabric of society and the quality of life in every industrial nation. The country that does this first will dominate the 21st century.—Peter Drucker

Transformational Strategies

CONCEPT 2.4
Leaders perceive themselves as leaders and choose to step up and transform themselves.

Purpose:

Our discussion of change and transformation are continued with concept 2.4, *Transformational Strategies*. In this section we will learn the basic strategies for moving into successful leadership.

Procedures:

- Use the following quote by Maccoley as a discussion starter. With the class, discuss the two basic traits Maccoley believes are important to successful leadership.

- Carefully discuss all materials leading up to activity 23.

- Complete activity 23 and discuss conclusions reached by students.

THE DEPARTURE POINT IS WANTING TO LEAD
AND BELIEVING THAT YOU CAN

Leaders are alike in their ability to bring together different types of people for a common goal, to transform adversarial competition into principled problem solving leading to consensus; character traits and action may differ from setting to setting. There is no one way to lead. —
Michael Maccoley

What we learn from Maccoley is the following:

- Leadership can be learned, and

- There is no one way to lead.

These two observations seem simple enough, but in reality, many people ignore them on their way to leadership positions. Understanding their importance is the *departure point* to becoming a leader. It begins with *believing that you can transform yourself into a leader.*

LEARNING TO LEAD REQUIRES UNDERSTANDING THAT LEADERSHIP DEVELOPMENT IS A PROCESS OF SELF-DEVELOPMENT

Leadership is a result of self-invention and the re-invention of self. Inventing oneself is the opposite of accepting the roles we are brought up to play. The process of self-invention starts with the internal focus of self-reflection and becomes a process of personal transformation. One of the first things we do in reflection is to question what is important in our lives. Goals grow out of our values, and we are motivated to achieve results that express our values and demonstrate what is important.—Warren Bennis

What we learn from Bennis is the following:

- The quest for leadership is a quest to discover who you are. Self-knowledge and self-invention result in self-development and all are a lifetime process.

- Leadership abilities always determine the effectiveness and potential impact on others. Personal and organizational effectiveness are proportionate to the strength of leadership.

We learn the following from John C. Maxwell (*The 21 Irrefutable Laws of Leadership,* 1998):

- The more we learn about leadership and the more my leadership behavior is characterized by what I have learned, the greater my success.

- Leadership ability always determines the effectiveness and potential impact I have on others.

- Leadership effectiveness requires that we raise our leadership knowledge and ability.

Maxwell points out that without leadership our organizational or corporate success is only about 35 percent. He also says that even if we lack leadership skills, we can move upward when we add commitment. Therefore:

LEADERSHIP LEARNING + COMMITMENT = SUCCESS

LEARNING TO LEAD REQUIRES A COMMITMENT TO ONGOING LEARNING

Reasons:

1. The moment we stop learning, we stop leading.

2. The moment we stop leading, we stop growing.

> **WE LEARN BEST WHEN WE TAKE RESPONSIBILITY FOR OUR OWN LEARNING.**

3. Interconnected forces of change are accelerating, causing forced obsolescence of skills and behaviors. Therefore, leaders must understand that dealing with change is not a *distraction* from their work, it *is* their work.

4. Power is no longer what we *know*, it is what we are willing to *learn*.

5. *Value* is no longer my specialty, it is how I *relate* my specialty to the whole.

The more our work makes us specialists, the more we must strive to become generalists in the work of others in order to gain knowledge of the interconnections. To avoid becoming lopsided or obsolete, we need to know as much as we can about everything if we intend to understand anything.—H. Darrell Young

LEARNING TO LEAD REQUIRES A NEW WAY OF
THINKING THAT CREATES MEANING FOR PEOPLE

Meaning has little to do with the facts or even knowing. Facts connote only information for the moment, and knowing uses these facts to perform particular behaviors. Meaning, on the other hand, has to do with thinking. It challenges old conventions by suggesting new directions and new visions. Meaning sees the world as a whole—simultaneously—as it is and as it can be. It understands the distinction between what is and what can be, using the ability to understand cause/effect relationships, to compare and contrast significant parts and changes, to hypothesize and predict, to prioritize and assess in order to make decisions and act on what is known and what is possible. Meaning and thinking bring unity to purpose, vision, and mission. In times of accelerated change, leaders will use their ability to think to focus on knowing why before knowing how and designing the future as they manage the present.

The ability to think, to conceptualize, and to remain open to environmental inputs is perhaps our greatest challenge. The challenges of the future will not wait for the intellectually unprepared nor the mentally timid. The future requires mentally flexible and critical thinkers. A basic assumption of general education is that the ability to reason lies at the heart of human intelligence.—Joe Hester, Teaching for Thinking, 1994

LEARNING TO LEAD IS ACHIEVED
ONE STEP AT A TIME

SMALL WINS LEAD TO MAJOR VICTORIES

- Therefore, we should incrementally break big issues into small, doable steps.

- We should also understand that small wins have huge benefits:

  ▶ Incremental commitments and small wins are at the heart of the change process, which promotes growth.

  ▶ Consistent patterns of winning build confidence and create excitement.

  ▶ Measurable ROI (return on investment) allows for constant feedback on results and recognition of what is important

> ▸ Small wins:

- Build faith in one's abilities and in those of others
- Encourage timely decision making, avoiding procrastination
- Maintain focus and encourage discipline
- Enables one to earn the right and walk before running
- Dictate continuous experimentation and innovation, yet control risks
- Allow recognition of individual contributions

SMALL WINS DEMONSTRATE CUSTOMER VALUE

- Small wins allow for balancing both tactical and strategic initiatives.

- Through small wins, empowerment is not overwhelming.

- Small wins allow one to discover one's improving abilities by experiencing success at different dimensions of the project.

- Small wins are the lifeblood of departments, groups, teams, classrooms, and those organized to develop innovative ideas and projects.

- Small wins keep hopes and determination alive.

- Small wins are vital because success breeds success.

LEARNING TO LEAD REQUIRES SACRIFICE
AND THE SACRIFICES ARE ONGOING

- Herein lies the answer to the question: "Where have all the leaders gone?" The cost of leadership is beyond what most people are willing to pay.

- As your leadership increases, your responsibilities increase and your rights decrease.

- Question: How would you prepare a leader for the toughest job assignment of the century? Examine the career of President Abraham Lincoln:

AGE:

22 Failed in business (1831)

23 Defeated for legislature

24 Second failure in business

26 Fiancée Ann Rutledge died

27 Suffered nervous breakdown

29 Defeated for speaker

31 Defeated for election

34 Defeated for Congress

39 Defeated for Congress

46 Defeated for Senate

47 Defeated for Vice President

49 Defeated for Senate

**52 Elected President of United
   States**

See: Donald T. Phillips, *Lincoln on Leadership*

A leader should always expect affirmation and deprivation. Often, solitude becomes a furnace for transformation.—H. Darrell Young

---

LEADERSHIP IS SHAPED BY ADVERSITY AND LEADERS ARE
MADE PERFECT THROUGH SUFFERING. IN DEVELOPING
LEADERSHIP ABILITY, THERE IS NO ON-TIME PAYMENT.

During his presidency, Lincoln agonized over the Civil War, took major shots from his cabinet and party, endured a bad marriage to a hysterical woman who nearly spent him into bankruptcy . . . and suffered endlessly when his favorite son, Willie, died before his tenth birthday.

We learn from Lincoln several important leadership lessons. Among these are the following:

- Leaders know what it is like to feel the desperate sense of hitting rock bottom. It is this feeling that many times creates the resilience needed to truly lead.

- Leaders must choose their responses to adversity and suffering. They may not be able to control circumstances, but they must control the way they face them.

- How did Lincoln handle adversity? What do you think was on his mind? When asked how he remained so cheerful in the face of constant adversity, he replied, "It's been my observation that people are just as happy as they make up their minds to be."

The strength of leadership can be measured by the number of scars on their backs.—Unknown

Don't despair, there is great news about true leaders: leaders emerge and do their best work as a result of adversity. They are made, self-made, and they invent themselves.

SUMMARY:

- Wanting to lead and believing that you can
- Understanding that leadership is a process of self-development
- Commitment to ongoing learning
- Thinking creates meaning for people
- Achievement comes one step at a time
- Sacrifice is ongoing

Activity 23: Transformational Strategies

Directions: Based on the six transformational strategies discussed in this section, outline a step-by-step plan for yourself and/or organization that states the behaviors/practices that must change for you to become more successful at what you now do:

1. _____

   _____

   _____

2. _____

   _____

   _____

3. _____

   _____

   _____

4. _____

   _____

   _____

5. _____

   _____

   _____

6. _____

   _____

   _____

THINGS TO REMEMBER

- Leaders choose to lead.

- Leadership development is a process of self-development.

- The moment you stop learning you stop leading.

- Leadership abilities always determine the effectiveness and potential impact on others; therefore, raise your ability to lead.

- Small wins, while learning how to become a leader, will lead to major victories.

- Leadership is shaped by adversity.

The Measurement of Transformation
Is Performance, Not Promises

CONCEPT 2.5
We lead by virtue of who we are and create value by virtue of our performance.

TO THE TEACHER

Purpose:

Performance evaluation is a major factor to maintaining performance quality and growth that fulfills the mission of the business or organization. This section concentrates on leadership measurement and assists with the defining of "quality performance" and the "value customers/ clients receive as a result."

Procedure:

- The teacher will have students concentrate on evaluating what is meant by "quality performance."

  - Review the two performance standards—quality and value—and then have students to complete activities 24 and 25.

  - The teacher will then review "Two Core Strategies for Achieving Quality Performance."

  - The teacher will then review the criteria for developing personal measurements and then engage students in activities 26 and 27. When completed, these should be reviewed with the whole class.

  - Review student responses with entire class and summarize with "Things to Remember."

PERFORMANCE STANDARDS: QUALITY AND VALUE

QUALITY: Performance, which is constant, provides results, which are constant,. The leadership needs to understand that the potential for better results is never realized. In fact, it is never understood!

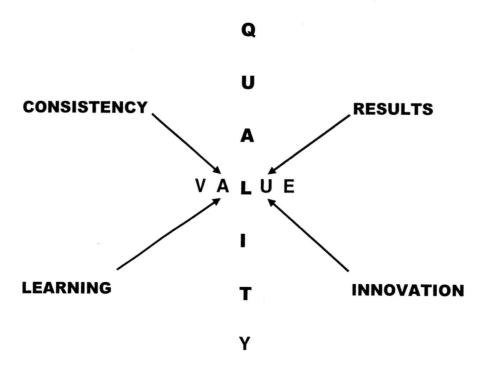

VALUE:

Our only sustainable competitive advantage in the future will be our ability to learn faster and innovate more quickly than the competition.—Michael Annison, *Managing the Whirlwind*

Activity 24: Transformational Strategies

Directions: In the space below, define what quality performance means to you. When you have completed your definitions, form groups of three to four students and give them time to share their individual definitions. Each group should work to gain consensus or agreement on a common definition of "quality performance." Each group will share its definition with the class.

Below are several examples to get you started:

- Only the best is worthy of our efforts
- Doing the right things right the first time
- Quality is ownership and pride
- Excellence and value
- Quality is flexibility and changing
- Quality is continuous improvement—what, who, whom
- Quality is an ongoing process; it is a journey

_____

_____

_____

_____

_____

_____

_____

_____

_____

_____

_____

_____

_____

_____

_____

Activity 25: Value Created as a Result of Quality Performance for Both the Internal and External Customer/Client

Directions: Examples of *value* created by quality performance are found in the left-hand column below. In the right-hand column, give examples of how each of these values might impact your work:

1. Organizations and individuals continually seek new and better ways of getting the job done.

2. We work differently by simplifying everything we do and developing measurements that encourage growth and loyalty rather than attempting to control employee initiative.

3. Standards will continue to rise.

4. Quality becomes everyone's business.

5. Quality initiatives are organized around the work to be done rather than the skills or interests of the people who do the work.

6. Time and patience are essential to the development of employee quality performance.

7. We give attention to shared values and goals, mutual respect and trust that enables employees to serve others rather than serving themselves or their departments.

Two Core Strategies

For Achieving Quality Performance

LINKING INTERNAL CUSTOMER/CLIENT SATISFACTION TO EXTERNAL CUSTOMER/CLIENT SATISFACTION

We begin with the first of these two core strategies: *linking internal customer/client satisfaction* and then move to *external satisfaction,* which is living up to customer perceptions and performing relative to expectations in the areas of service, product, crises, complaints, delivery, costs, and effectiveness. There are two types of customers: (1) those within the organization (internal) whose performance we value, and (2) those customers to whom and for whom we direct our service (external). REMEMBER: We can never have external customer satisfaction until we have collective internal satisfaction.

Understanding the Problem

Following is an example of internal and external customer satisfaction as applied to the public schools. You can apply this to your own life and work by following these examples.

INTERNAL CUSTOMER:

The reference here is to employees; in schools these are teachers, principals, supervisors, superintendents, cafeteria workers, secretaries, and teacher assistants, etc. Internal satisfaction means that schools, like businesses, must create internal leadership development systems. As Schlechty (1990) says, "Teachers are, of necessity, part of a 'corporate' structure, and their effectiveness is at least partly determined by the way the 'corporations' in which they work are organized and managed" (143). Among other things, this means creating an organization that supports human resource development, school improvement, and leadership development activities.

EXTERNAL CUSTOMER:

The external customers of the schools are the students who come to be educated there. The schools must be accountable for the results of student education, but we must caution that students are knowledge workers and their education should be tailored for work in a knowledge and service-oriented environment. If we wish to serve this customer effectively, then we must move from viewing student learning and the results of student learning as products to viewing student learning as a process that is just beginning and will last a lifetime. In fact, students need to be challenged, not as information consumers, but as knowledge producers whose schoolwork is meaningful and engaging. To serve this student, schools should be a place where teachers and students have increased opportunities for success, as Schlechty comments, "schools in which every teacher is a leader, every leader is a teacher, and every student is a success" (137).

LOOSING THE CONNECTION BETWEEN INTERNAL AND EXTERNAL CUSTOMER:

The greater the commitment to knowledge/education, the more specialized resources become. The value connection between internal and external customers is changing as knowledge increases and customers become more specialized in both their skills and jobs. Let me give you an example that is presently occurring within the medical profession as a result of technological advancement: more information leads to more knowledge and more knowledge leads to greater technological advancement that eventually leads to specialized resources and services. The chart below shows that when more specialization is added to service, there is loss of contact between the professionals and those whom they serve. This also means the further the service is removed from the customer, the more dependent we become on each other's specialization.

A friend once said that he went into the hospital for a simple colon examination. A week later he received a bill from the gastrologist, another from the anesthesiologist, another from the pathologist, and an additional statement from his internist who was sent the results. Although these doctors were dependent on each other's expertise, my friend said that he only met the gastrologist briefly and never met the anesthesiologist or the pathologist.

Built into the Information Age is a requirement of interdependence on each other for value and success. Power is no longer individual knowledge. Today it is how effectively I can apply any knowledge to that of others. The issue we face is that our value is constantly changing and becoming obsolete. Driven by a faster pace than ever before—as knowledge and customer expectations and needs increase—my personal value is now my ability to apply my individual knowledge to that of others to resolve problems and advance achievement.

Consider the following example of how moving from the patient to more specialized medical care increases the dependence of the patient on the interconnections of specializations:

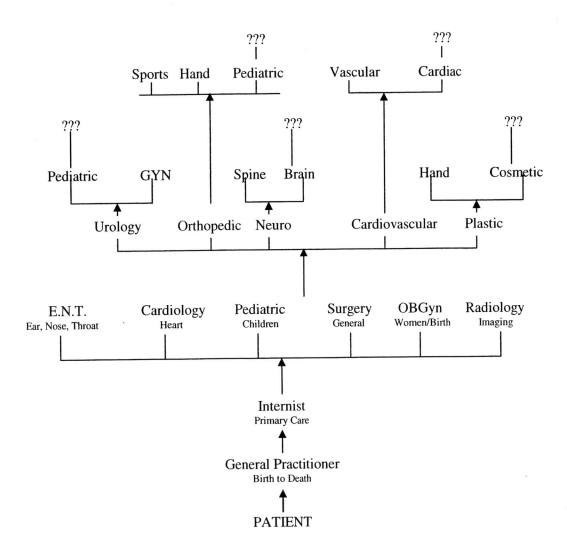

Evaluating the Problem

RULES FOR ACHIEVING CUSTOMER SATISFACTION

RANK THE FOLLOWING RULES 1–5 IN ORDER OF IMPORTANCE, WITH 5 BEING "MOST IMPORTANT." CIRCLE THE ANSWER YOU CHOOSE:

1 2 3 4 5   • You can't be all things to all people.

1 2 3 4 5   • You are not effectively serving your customers unless there is an entire group that doesn't like what you do and how you do it.

1 2 3 4 5   • Recognize the differences between acquiring customers and retaining customers.

1 2 3 4 5   • Customers fall into one of two different categories; they're either apostles or terrorists.

1 2 3 4 5   • Walk in your customers' shoes; understand and manage the encounter from beginning to end.

1 2 3 4 5   • Ask your customers what they want. Unless you have customer data, managers talking to managers about customer needs are a waste of time.

1 2 3 4 5   • Establish the value of your customer. Manage as a long-term relationship, not as a transaction.

1 2 3 4 5   • Don't let service and business outcomes get in opposition to each other.

1 2 3 4 5   • People who serve other people do not have a lower station in life.

1 2 3 4 5   • The closer you get to the customer; the priority must be service over financial results.

1 2 3 4 5   • Finally, find out who your customers are, what they want and need, and provide it for them.

Solving the Problem

The value of my (the leader's) knowledge is how it can be applied to the value of others. Keep this in mind as you complete activities 26 and 27 on the following pages.

Activity 26: Linking the Internal/External Customer

Directions: Using the words listed below, develop a service chain (flowchart) that sequences the events that drive the purposes of business:

WORDS

Internal service quality/employee value
Leadership
External service quality/customer value
Employee satisfaction
Customer loyalty

Profit
Employee loyalty
Growth
Customer satisfaction

LEADERSHIP

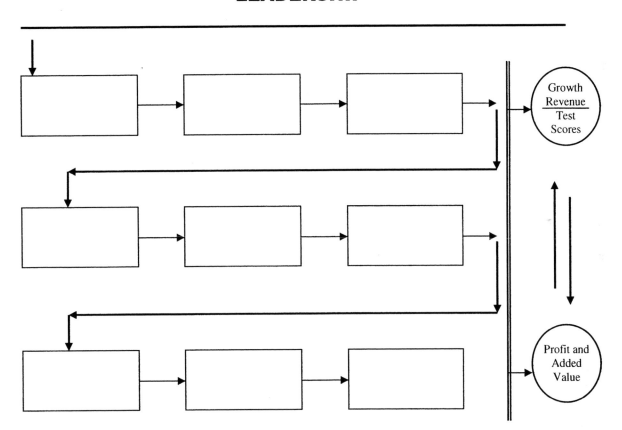

Activity 27: Growth and Transformation

Directions: Briefly describe how each of the concepts below contributes to the growth of the organization. Check your responses with those on the next page and discuss the similarities and differences that you perceive.

Leadership

    _____

Internal Service Quality/
Employee Value

Employee Satisfaction

Employee Loyalty

External Service Quality/
Customer Value

Customer Satisfaction

Customer Loyalty

Revenue Growth and Profit

SERVING THE INTERNAL AND EXTERNAL CUSTOMER

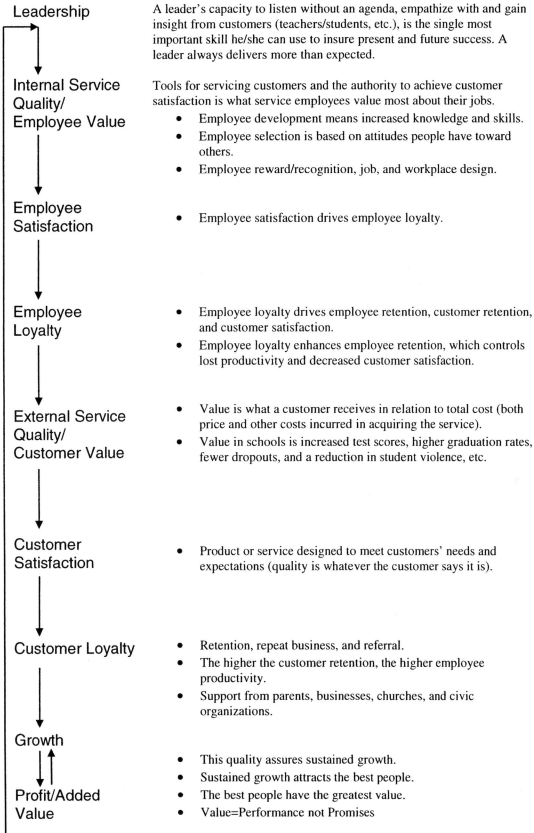

Leadership

A leader's capacity to listen without an agenda, empathize with and gain insight from customers (teachers/students, etc.), is the single most important skill he/she can use to insure present and future success. A leader always delivers more than expected.

Internal Service Quality/ Employee Value

Tools for servicing customers and the authority to achieve customer satisfaction is what service employees value most about their jobs.
- Employee development means increased knowledge and skills.
- Employee selection is based on attitudes people have toward others.
- Employee reward/recognition, job, and workplace design.

Employee Satisfaction

- Employee satisfaction drives employee loyalty.

Employee Loyalty

- Employee loyalty drives employee retention, customer retention, and customer satisfaction.
- Employee loyalty enhances employee retention, which controls lost productivity and decreased customer satisfaction.

External Service Quality/ Customer Value

- Value is what a customer receives in relation to total cost (both price and other costs incurred in acquiring the service).
- Value in schools is increased test scores, higher graduation rates, fewer dropouts, and a reduction in student violence, etc.

Customer Satisfaction

- Product or service designed to meet customers' needs and expectations (quality is whatever the customer says it is).

Customer Loyalty

- Retention, repeat business, and referral.
- The higher the customer retention, the higher employee productivity.
- Support from parents, businesses, churches, and civic organizations.

Growth

Profit/Added Value

- This quality assures sustained growth.
- Sustained growth attracts the best people.
- The best people have the greatest value.
- Value=Performance not Promises

Adapted from: J. L. Heskett and L. A. Schlesinger, et al., *Harvard Business Review*, March/April 1994; modified to include schools, etc.

DEVELOP PERSONAL MEASUREMENT FOR CONTINUOUS IMPROVEMENT
A FOCUS ON VALUE AND OUTCOMES
RATHER THAN NICKELS AND NOSES

We have learned that what gets measured gets done. We have also learned that the goal of measurement and of personal accountability is to develop, not to trap. Entrapment and measurement are neither compatible nor do they serve the same purpose. Measurement looks beyond symptoms to root causes and identifies areas needing attention such as employee training or rebuilding practices that enrich customer service in more efficient ways.

THOSE WHO MEASURE AND THOSE BEING MEASURED MUST:

- Understand what is being measured.

- Focus on reinvention, character, innovation, entrepreneurship, adaptability, knowledge, skills, and problem solving.

- Know why it is being measured.

- Understand who is responsible for doing the measuring, and why.

- Know who will take action and what action will be taken.

- Integrate individual needs with organizational goals to ensure measurement as a tool for development and growth.

Following are sets of competencies for measurement and growth that were developed by HBO & Company in 1987. They are organized around the following practices:

- UNITY WITHOUT UNIFORMITY

- TRANSFORMANCE, NOT PROMISES

- LEADERS GROWING LEADERS

The time has come to develop the principles, the practices, and the disciplines of innovation and entrepreneurship. The emergence of the entrepreneurial society may be a major turning point in history.—Peter Drucker

UNITY WITHOUT UNIFORMITY

Diagnostic Use of Concepts—describes people who are able to connect previously conceived concepts to explain and interpret current situations. They are able to differentiate real versus apparent problems, relevant versus irrelevant information, and have a good sense of when to act independently and when to refer to a higher authority.

Conceptualize and Communicate Big Picture—describes people who are creative, innovative, and visionary. They have the ability to clearly picture and communicate, with insight and meaning, a "new way" to others.

Use of Oral Presentations—describes people with good communication and presentation skills. It not only refers to capability, but to quality, delivery, and the visual or sound aids that are used. Most importantly, it refers to the talent to question listeners to make certain that individuals understand the message.

Logical Thought—describes systematic thinking, which is used to solve complex problems, prioritize information, make difficult decisions, and understand cause and effect relationships.

Self-Confidence—describes people who convey their belief in themselves to do good work without being arrogant or defensive. A person who is consistently decisive and self-assured in a variety of situations is self-confident.

TRANSFORMANCE NOT PROMISES

Efficiency—describes those who are efficient and continually strive to improve methods and practices, using as a measurement previous personal performance, the performance of others, or a standard of excellence. These people think in terms of results. They set goals, plan, prioritize, and organize their resources to maximize return on investment by increasing efficiency and productivity.

Self-Control—describes those who possess self-control and who are able to defer personal desires or needs in the service of organizational needs. They consider both the liabilities and benefits to themselves and the organization before expressing or acting on personal needs and desires. They resist responding angrily or defensively when verbally attacked or confronted by another. People who are self-controlled are also self-disciplined, self-confident, and are logical thinkers.

Stamina and Adaptability—describes those who perform well and behave calmly and patiently under stress. They are flexible and adaptable in changing their course of action according to changing job demands, environment, or changes within the organization. During times of change, they maintain their quality performance, attention to detail, and a high level of energy.

Accurate Self-Assessment—describes individuals who are cognizant of their strengths, weaknesses, and limitations. They can articulate and assess their performance and are committed to learning activities to improve themselves.

Pro-Activity—describes those who show initiative and take action to get something accomplished. A skillful problem solver who takes risks, accepts personal responsibility and accountability, seeks information on his or her own and responds in a task-sequenced way rather than reacting to the situation as it evolves.

Concern with Impact (Pride in Work)—describes those who project a self-image that says, "I am important." These people explicitly express concern with their reputation and image and the reputation and image of their organization and its services and products.

LEADERS GROWING LEADERS

Directing Others—describes those who use their influence to obtain the cooperation, compliance, or support of others. These persons are decisive in decision making and enforce rules and procedures to obtain the cooperation of others.

Developing Others—describes those who help others do their jobs, which results in improved performance, greater productivity, and retention of good people. They give performance feedback on a regular basis, provide necessary resources, and encourage team members to openly discuss problems and take responsibility for the outcomes.

Spontaneity—describes those who are mature and secure enough to openly and freely express opinions, feelings, and thoughts without excessive forethought or worrying about the impact of their actions.

Team-Builder—describes those who use influence to build coalitions, teams, alliances, and networks—whether a leader or a member of those groups. They model desirable team behaviors and influence others to act the same.

Managing Group Process—describes those who inspire others to work effectively in groups. They clearly communicate the need for cooperation, mission, and teamwork within and between work groups. They delegate tasks rather than performing alone. They involve all concerned individuals in the resolution of work-unit-conflict and create symbols of group identity, trust, and pride.

Positive Regard—describes those who communicate a positive belief in others. They tell others when performance is up to the expectations of superiors and let them know when change and improvements are needed.

Objectivity—describes those who view situations and people in an objective manner and from multiple perspectives. They have the ability to explain another's point of view when it differs from their own, and are able to list the pros and cons of alternative options and decisions. They also acknowledge the injured feelings of anyone negatively impacted by action taken for the good of the organization.

Activity 28: The Measurements

Directions: Review the competencies on the previous pages, then summarize your strengths and weaknesses in each competency:

Diagnostic Use of Concepts: _____

_____

_____

Conceptualize and Communicate
the Big Picture: _____

_____

Use of Oral Presentations: _____

_____

Logical Thought: _____

_____

Self-Confidence: _____

_____

Efficiency: _____

_____

Self-Control: _____

_____

Stamina and Adaptability: _____

_____

Accurate Self-Assessment: _____

                                     _____

                                     _____

Pro-Activity: _____

                                     _____

Concern with Impact   _____
(Pride in Work):
                                     _____

                                     _____

Directing Others: _____

                                     _____

                                     _____

Developing Others: _____

                                     _____

                                     _____

Spontaneity: _____

                                     _____

                                     _____

Team-Builder: _____

                                     _____

                                     _____

Manages Group Processes: _____

                                     _____

                                     _____

Positive Regard: _____

                                     _____

                                     _____

Objectivity: _____

                                     _____

                                     _____

Activity 29: Personal Assessment

Directions: Now that you have summarized your strengths and weaknesses in each competency, choose three that you consider to be your best. Also, choose three that you believe are your weakest and that you need to work on. Beside each of these competencies, tell why you are good at it or why you are not so good at it. In the second part of this exercise—"How Might I Improve My Weaknesses?"—tell what you can do to improve your chosen three competencies. Discuss in small groups and with the class.

STRONG COMPETENCIES:

1. _____

_____

_____

_____

2. _____

_____

_____

_____

3. _____

_____

_____

_____

WEAK COMPETENCIES:

1. _____

_____

_____

_____

2. _____

_____

_____

_____

3. _____

_____

_____

_____

HOW MIGHT I IMPROVE MY WEAKNESSES?

Use this space to list ways to improve your weaknesses:

THINGS TO REMEMBER

- Words may be used in an attempt to define quality, but actions and final results are the only true definition.

- Quality performance means changing our definition of the customer, customer service, customer satisfaction, and loyalty.

- In order to insure external customer satisfaction and value, you must first achieve internal customer satisfaction and value.

- If you are trying to respond to the needs of a particular population by talking to someone else, don't be surprised when you fail.

BUILDING RELATIONSHIPS

Building a Leadership Culture

Building a Leadership Culture is about creating an environment and culture where leaders divest themselves and invest in others.

PART 3 EMPHASIZES THREE FUNDAMENTAL CONCEPTS:

Cornerstones for Developing Leaders

The Leaders New Work

Divesting and Investing

BUILDING A LEADERSHIP CULTURE

Linking Performance to Relationships

THE CONCEPT OF "LEADERSHIP"

Several years ago Darrell Young met with Warren Bennis to discuss the practice of leadership. He asked Mr. Bennis if he had to choose one word that best describes "leadership," what word would he choose? Bennis answered, "Darrell, I wish it were that simple." In the discussion that followed, Bennis explained that vision and influence are at the top of his list, but that neither would be possible without first *defining and understanding current realities and the development of sustainable, quality relationships.* Implied by these comments is that we cannot change current realities without letting go of the present and we cannot have sustainable quality relationships without expanding ethical behaviors. Leadership worth following is built on these two concepts.

Part 3 focuses on these leadership concepts and behaviors required for creating a leadership culture through the development and expansion of sustainable quality relationships. Part 3 also introduces significant leadership applications. Experience has taught us that a leadership culture flows quite naturally from environments where leaders choose to invest in followers for the purpose of creating a successor generation of leaders. Within this environment, leaders choose to invest in followers for the purpose of creating leaders for the future. By doing this, present leaders become more effective: institutionalizing a leadership-centered culture is the ultimate act of leadership.

In this workbook we learn that influence is determined by relationships and that the primary requirements for building and supporting relationships are accepting individual differences and living an ethical life. Over time, we become acutely aware of the difficulties and complexities of sustaining these two requirements. The cadence of our leadership growth will find consistency in our ability to accept people as they are—not as we would like them to be, in living an ethical life, and in our willingness to give significant amounts of time in the service of others. What we will learn is that becoming an influential and effective leader requires working with other leaders who also work with other leaders. We cannot take the vision forward alone. Leadership is about multiplying our efforts, which will automatically multiply our results.

Staying on this point for a minute, Darrell Young says that one of the most interesting conversations he has had with high school students concerns the connection between personal growth and other people. Once we reach the conclusion that we cannot grow without the support of others, knowledge of the strengths, weaknesses, and competencies of those from whom we learn the most becomes apparent. Our friends, colleagues, and family hold the keys to our future success. As Zander and Zander comment in their book *The Art of Possibility,* "On the whole, resources are likely to come to you in greater abundance when you are generous and inclusive and engage people in your passion for life. There aren't any guarantees, of course. When you are oriented to abundance, you care less about being in control, and you take more risks. . . . In the measurement of the world, you set a goal and strive for it. In the universe of possibility, you set the context and let life unfold."

Building a leadership culture requires us to generate great strength from within, but it is the strength we receive from others that enables and sustains our vision. We are what we are, what we hope for, what we imagine, and what we are committed to work for. Nothing comes easy, and, in this life, nothing is cheap. It takes a great deal of effort to overcome the barriers culture and societies have placed in our path. Success will come and we learn that it is more of a group process than an individual accomplishment—an ongoing commitment with no end in sight. It is this commitment that is the source of our value.

When we stand back and look at our world from afar, we realize that value is continually created, that it is not a shrinking pie, and that human beings can share in and accelerate the growth of value through work, art, education, and religion. Positive value creates community and it is with others that we are able to increase the well-being of mankind. Negative value negates human value and belittles the dignity of individual life. It is positive value that should circulate freely where it is needed. Great leaders create value by putting themselves in the service of others. They create learning environments through which there is continual growth and improvement.

The moment a leader steps away from his/her strengths and core competencies, his/her effectiveness as a leader is diminished, as well as the quality of the followers he will attract. The performance of the organization and the development of the organization's learning culture will always be enhanced when the leader utilizes his/her strengths and delegates his /her weaknesses. John Seed, in his book, *Thinking Life a Mountain,* reminds us that when we "think like a mountain," we are no longer isolated but connected to a much larger environmental whole. Understanding our essential relationship to employees and colleagues in no way diminishes our leadership position or capacity. Some have called this particular perspective "the ecological self." It does not mean that our individuality and uniqueness are insignificant. Rather, what it means is that we should experience the organization as a part of us and the story of its employees as our own extended life story. This experience has a unifying affect and allows us to be creative within a larger concept of whom we are—the possible human that lies within.

Within the ecology of effective organizations there is group dynamic or rhythm that supports and maintains its energy and importance. Learning is occurring, weaknesses are being turned into strengths, and competition is ongoing. Leaders at the top and in departments and groups will enhance and encourage the growth of others and, at times, follow those whose skills and energies have come together to promote the higher vision and purpose of the organization. Great leaders always know when to follow.

High school students in our training courses have said, "Leadership is where the rubber meets the road." That is, the leadership journey helps us define who we are and what we are striving to become. It sets a direction of where we want to go and begins the process of establishing the rules for continuous improvement. As our leadership journey continues, keep the following in mind: a friend sharpens a friend and whoever walks with the wise will become wise. Based on present-day events in business, athletics, education, and politics, it is not difficult to understand the need for a new generation of leaders, leaders who are committed to ethical principles and serving others. Understanding the principles of ethical and servant leadership enables us to grow in our leadership capability. Knowledge, new skills, networking, and a commitment to leadership development add value as they are appropriately applied to the organization's needs.

ICE-BREAKERS

Want to lead with purpose? Serve with your whole heart.—Joe Eastman

The goal of interpersonal mastery is to shift our focus from self-fulfillment to one of service-fulfillment. It is centered in purpose—how we can serve others to make a difference in the world.
—Kevin Cashman

Leaders follow in order to lead by managing themselves, managing change, and serving others, which regenerates the ability to lead.—Joe Hester

Cultivating the Foundations for Developing Leaders

CONCEPT 3.1
Leadership cornerstones will determine your success in creating a leadership culture where other leaders emerge.

Purpose:

The purpose of this section is to review the basic principles for hiring and developing your leadership cornerstones to insure a strong foundation from which to build a culture where leaders emerge.

Procedures:

- Begin by reviewing concept 3.1; then ask participants what is meant by "intellectual capital."

- Review and discuss the three requirements for leadership-foundation building: strategic thinking, continuous improvement, and building relationships.

- Have students read chapter 5 in *Ethical Leadership*. They should get a firm grip on the concept of "empowerment" as "enabling the performance of others" before moving on.

- Participants should answer all the questions at the end of chapter 5 in *Ethical Leadership* before moving into the activities of this section.

Activities:

- Students will complete activities 31–35. Discuss and share results with the class.

ATTRACTING AND RECRUITING THE RIGHT PEOPLE

The objective of this section is to evaluate and think through the criteria for attracting and recruiting organizational cornerstones that will help establish a culture where successor generations of leaders emerge and mission fulfills purpose. Retaining and developing a leadership foundation is hard work, however, and we must never stop improving our foundation. The development and sustainability of the culture depends on those closest to us. An exercise that I often use to stimulate discussion and thought regarding this objective is to ask that the following sentences be completed:

- We want to work in organizations that value

- This organization values

- These people value

Everyone plays a role in determining personal and organizational value. Without a leadership framework, the culture will evolve on its own and will probably become dysfunctional resulting in individual fiefdoms where people are aggressive, competitive, jealous, paranoid about positions, and generally distrustful. Obviously this is not a leadership culture, nor is it a culture where we wish to work. Therefore, never underestimate the importance and power of attracting and recruiting the "right people."

Leaders, especially those who are attracting and recruiting others to the organization, should evaluate what they believe to be their core competencies and skills (see part 2) before trying to choose their team. When a leader effectively evaluates his/her own competencies, this evaluation should determine what core leadership competencies and skills are needed for a balanced team.

The consensus that we need is a consensus in which many voices are heard and in which those voices remain distinct, yet all are voices, if you like, in the same choir.—Danah Sohar and Ian Marshall, *The Quantum Society*

DETERMINING CORE COMPETENCIES

In any business, self-evaluation is extremely important and necessary for continuous growth and leadership improvement. Leaders who believe they are good at everything cease to grow. Improvement becomes irrelevant. When we recognize and understand our strengths and weaknesses, we are in a better position to learn from others and to recruit to our organization those who will complement our strengths and shore up our weaknesses.

We identify these individuals as "the right people" for our organization. Self-evaluation allows us to capitalize on their strengths in performance, learning, and growth opportunities. We all have core competencies, some of which can be improved upon through training and coaching. Of course, there are some core competencies that some of us will never possess in their entirety. Effective leaders are able to identify these two areas—core competencies that can be improved upon and core competencies that we may never improve upon to the degree needed in the organization. The important matter is to avoid being devoured by those competencies that lay outside our ability to completely master.

The principle is quite simple: leaders need to position themselves to do less and accomplish more by understanding their personal strengths and weaknesses and delegating those tasks that other team members are better qualified to perform. Another advantage of self-evaluation and understanding is that the leader is able to identify those areas in which he or she is most likely to add value to the organization. This will enable the leader to leverage his or her leadership competencies and skills to the best advantage of the organization's purpose and goals. When the leader consistently steps away from his or her core competencies, his or her leadership effectiveness is diminished. The leader also loses the respect and devotion of team members as the potential shared learning and growth from within the organization becomes limited. Everyone suffers from those who claim "position power" and "role arrogance."

A balanced organization in which everyone is challenged and allowed to exercise core competencies focuses on organizational strengths and empowers members at each layer of the organization to do the same. Many times leaders make a fallacious assumption that because they are in a "position" of leadership, their core competencies are all encompassing. Everyone in the organization benefits when tasks are delegated by recognized strengths and when others are empowered to act and are given the responsibility and authority to make decisions within the domain of their strengths.

Leadership cultures require that leaders identify the core competencies of all team members and commit themselves to the continuous upgrading of their performance and the performance of others. The responsibility is arduous, but the task is simple: leaders are more effective who work within their strengths and delegate tasks that expose their weaknesses.

Activity 30: Recruiting Leaders—Know Your Competencies

Directions: Review the list of competencies in part 2, pages 122–124. It is vital that leaders understand and identify their strengths and weaknesses. Underline those competencies in each column that you consider strengths and circle those that you consider weaknesses.

UNITY WITHOUT UNIFORMITY	TRANSFORMANCE NOT PROMISES	LEADERS GROWING LEADERS
DIAGNOSTIC USE OF CONCEPTS	EFFICIENCY	DIRECTING OTHERS
CONCEPTUALIZE AND COMMUNICATE BIG PICTURE	SELF-CONTROL	DEVELOPING OTHERS
USE OF ORAL PRESENTATIONS	STAMINA AND ADAPTABILITY	SPONTANEITY
LOGICAL THOUGHT	ACCURATE SELF-ASSESSMENT	TEAM-BUILDER
SELF-CONFIDENCE	PRO-ACTIVITY	MANAGING GROUP PROCESS
	CONCERN WITH IMPACT (PRIDE IN WORK)	POSITIVE REGARD
		OBJECTIVITY

Activity 31: Achieving Organizational Balance Evaluation Sheet

Directions: Review the problem-situation below. When your review is finished, complete the evaluation form that follows.

Problem-situation: As the CEO of your organization, you must interview and hire a head of your research and development department. Based on your self-evaluation in activity 30, prioritize (with 1 being the highest and 6 being the lowest) the competencies needed for this departmental head. When completed, explain your choices and discuss with the class.

1–6	UNITY WITHOUT UNIFORMITY	1–6	TRANSFORMANCE NOT PROMISES	1–6	LEADERS GROWING LEADERS
	DIAGNOSTIC USE OF CONCEPTS		EFFICIENCY		DIRECTING OTHERS
			SELF-CONTROL		DEVELOPING OTHERS
	CONCEPTUALIZE AND COMMUNICATE BIG PICTURE		STAMINA AND ADAPTABILITY		SPONTANEITY
	USE OF ORAL PRESENTATIONS		ACCURATE SELF-ASSESSMENT		TEAM-BUILDER
			PRO-ACTIVITY		MANAGING GROUP PROCESS
	LOGICAL THOUGHT		CONCERN WITH IMPACT (PRIDE IN WORK)		POSITIVE REGARD
	SELF-CONFIDENCE				OBJECTIVITY

Explanation:

Once you have completed the two activities from the previous page, review the additional criteria below for attracting and recruiting the right people to your organization. These ten additional areas provide you with additional areas of consideration. Building a balanced and well-functioning team is an ongoing process and is not to be taken lightly.

ADDITIONAL CRITERIA AND TOPICS FOR CONSIDERATION

CRITERIA

1. Compatibility: Know where and how they fit with other team members.

2. Appreciation: Respect, care, and trust team members.

3. Value: Team members—new and old—must understand and be able to articulate their value to the team and the larger organization.

4. Community: Let individuals know they are needed.

5. Creativity: The working environment is flexible, open, and allows for innovation.

6. Rewards: Recognition and rewards are provided for significant achievement.

7. Mentoring: Team members must embrace a mentoring philosophy.

8. Assessment: Assessment is ongoing and relevant to the organization's mission. Achievement benchmarks are provided.

9. Connect: Ongoing training should demonstrate the relevancy of skills, discovery, and problem solving.

10. Talent: Make sure talented team members are recruited that can do things others—including the leader—cannot do.

DISCUSSION TOPICS

1. Leaders must choose people who agree with where they—the leaders—are going, and exhibit trust that the leaders will get them there (see part 1of this book).

2. Those closest to a leader determine the leader's potential. Consider:

    • Those who are internally motivated need little external prodding for achieving excellence.

- Organizational and team cheerleaders keep motivation and morale high when the going gets tough.

- Those who seek to improve themselves through continuous learning are always improving those around them; they become the organization's teachers.

- Those who have special talents and/or skills and, who recognize the talents and skills of others are willing to learn and are great team players.

- A leadership culture is built by those who are willing to learn, share what they have learned, and seek to complement the talents of others.

(Adapted from: John Maxwell, *The 21 Irrefutable Laws of Leadership*, p. 115)

3. Evaluate the following statements with reference to "getting the job done":

- Never confuse competency with skill.

- Never confuse purpose with mission.

- Never confuse goal incentives with personal growth.

Activity 32: Evaluating the People in Your Organization

Directions: Give the people in your organization nicknames, including yourself. Put these nicknames in either column 1, 2, or 3 according to how you think they respond to leadership.

ACCEPT	NOT SURE	NEGATIVE

Activity 33: Building an Organization

Directions: If you were/are the leader of your organization and felt it necessary to choose cornerstones of committed individuals, who would you pick? Using nicknames, make your choices and place them in one—or more than one—of the five categories below:

INTERNALY MOTIVATED	TEAM CHEER-LEADERS	CONSTANT LEARNERS	HAVE SPECIAL TALENTS AND SKILLS	TEAM-ORIENTED

RETAINING AND IMPROVING THE
LEADERSHIP FOUNDATION

1. Retaining and improving leaders is hard work, but we must never stop improving.

Consider the following criteria for retaining and improving your leadership foundation:

- **Recognizing:**   Recognize that talented people are your greatest asset.

- **Clarifying:**   Define performance rather than spending time trying to enhance performance.

- **Teaming:**   Put good talent with top talent.

- **Motivating:**   Promote good work and assign "mission impossibles."

- **Investing:**   Employ and develop intellectual capital.

- **Placing:**   Insure that the right person is in the right job and has the right tools.

- **Honoring:**   Have the courage to retain the right people.

2. Building a leadership culture depends, in large part, on how you value others.

(Emphasized by John Maxwell, *The 21 Irrefutable Laws of Leadership,* 'The Law of Explosive Growth')

- **LEADERS WHO DEVELOP FOLLOWERS**

  - Need to be needed

  - Hold on to power

  - Spend time with others

  - Grow by addition

  - Focus on weaknesses

- **LEADERS WHO DEVELOP LEADERS**

- Want to be succeeded

- Give power away

- Invest time with others

- Grow by multiplication

- Focus on strengths

Activity 34: Improving the Foundation

Directions: What strategies can you think of for improving your foundation (your character, skills, competencies, etc.)? How can we make improvements in our foundation at every level? Describe your "foundation" in one or two key words and place in the middle circle. In the second circle, brainstorm and list the strategies for improving your foundation. Finally, in the outer box, list the resources you think you will need for achieving your goals.

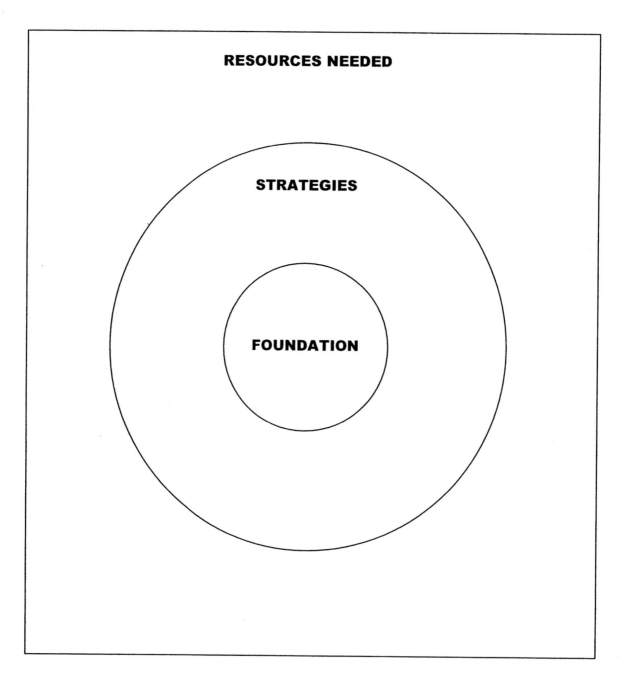

BUILDING A CULTURE FOR SUCCESSION

1. It takes a leader to grow a leader.

85%

of all potential leaders come from

the influence of other leaders.

(See: Maxwell, 1998, pp. 6–7)

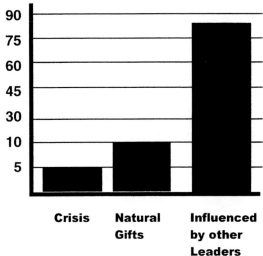

According to Warren Bennis, few leaders (only about five percent) are appointed due to a crisis in the organization. A few more individuals make the leadership ranks because of their natural talents and special skills. Bennis points out that the vast majority of leaders (around eighty-five percent) rise up through the organization through networking with colleagues and by building positive, trusting relationships with them.

The leader finds greatness in the group, and he or she helps the members find it in themselves.
—Warren Bennis

Reasons leaders don't grow other leaders

- They don't recognize the value of growing other leaders.

- They focus attention on developing followers rather than leaders.

- They are insecure and fear replacement.

- They focus too much on their personal leadership development.

- They haven't evaluated their own leadership style and development.

Leaders don't divest of themselves and invest in others to develop a few good men or women. They divest and invest to create a successor generation.—H. Darrell Young

2. It takes courage to establish your leadership.

- Courage to face current reality and not pretend things are different than they really are.

- Courage not to ignore constructive criticism.

- Courage not to isolate yourself as a result of decision making.

- Courage to remain focused on progress, managing change, taking risks, and facing uncertainity.

3. It takes clarity of purpose to deal with environmental and cultural uncertainty.

Uncertainty

- Uncertainty is a permanent reality with leadership.

- The greater the uncertainty the greater the need for leadership.

- The more responsibility the more uncertainty leaders must manage.

- Leadership responsibilities are capped by our ability or inability to manage uncertainty.

- With success comes greater uncertainty.

Certainty

- It is not the leader's responsibility to remove uncertainty; it is, however, his or her responsibility to bring clarity into the midst of the uncertain dilemma.

- Clarity results in influence.

- Leaders can be wrong but they cannot be unclear.

- Clarity of vision will sometimes compensate for uncertainty in planning.

4. It takes *multiplication* to create a culture for succession.

Leaders who grow followers add to their organization one person at a time. Leaders who grow leaders, *multiply* their growth because they get those leaders as followers.

THINGS TO REMEMBER

- A weak foundation will eventually crack and fall.

- Who you are is who you will attract.

- It takes a leader to grow a leader.

- Leaders who develop leaders experience incredible multiplication.

- Those who determine a leader's potential are the closest to him/her.

Activity 35: Building Relationships

Narrative: We discuss building relationships to illustrate the dynamics of building an ethical culture within the organization that connects reasoning, conduct, and character. It is an understatement to say that relationship building is difficult to maintain throughout the organization. Organizational energy is often directed toward issues of conflict and cooperation, and the movement to resolve conflict and sustain cooperation is an essential element in this process.

That people within an organization change from day to day is a given fact of life. Issues involving home, job location, relations with coworkers, and job satisfaction or dissatisfaction are just a few of the variables that move people to behave in one way or another. Leaders need to practice patience and exercise flexibility when dealing with different people in the organization. Leaders at every level also need to recognize the volatility of personality and mood changes among its people. This is a major reason that relationship building is so difficult.

The graphic below illustrates the three significant elements in building and maintaining a leadership culture:

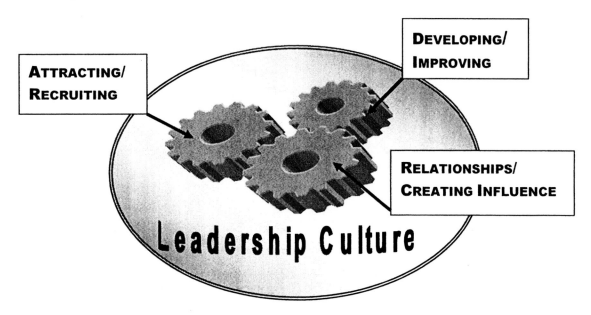

Two concepts emerge in our discussion of relationship building. They are the following:

- Know both your internal and external customers.

- Know that both of these will—over time—undergo significant change.

Building relationships is hard work!

Time is like a river made up of the events that happen and its current is strong; no sooner does anything appear than it is swept away, and another comes in its place, and will be swept away too.—Marcus Aurelius Antoninums, *Meditations*

Directions: As a leader, it is important to understand that building and sustaining positive relationships within the organization begins with self-understanding. Human action has four basic dimensions: *lived experience, social experience, cultural experience,* and *creative experience.* In the spaces provided below, answer the following questions:

Lived Experience: How has becoming a leader in your organization changed your perception of others? Be specific.

Social Experience: Do you recognize and honor individual differences throughout your organization and, at the same time, seek a common ground on which to build a common bond with others? Explain.

Cultural Experience: Have you drawn on the shared ideas, beliefs, and experiences of the organization through reason and a common moral code to provide a foundation for developing a learning culture? Give examples.

Creative Experience: While cultural experience is the generation and use of objects, ideas, and beliefs created in the past, creative experience is the generation and use of new objects, ideas, and beliefs. Creative experience is future oriented.

Question: In what ways have you encouraged the development of unrestricted/organic relationships that encourage the development of unique and different ideas for the advancement and enhancement of the common purposes of the organization? Give several examples.

In the "test" below—used by permission: Dr. Dwight "Ike" Reighard, *Discovering Your North Star*, Quantum Leap Publishing, 1998—students should be given fifteen minutes to read and mark their answers in the fifteen self-evaluation categories. Students will select one answer (a–d) in each category. When given to the same group at a later time, you may find that they answer differently than they did before. This is not a personality test. It is intended to demonstrate how difficult it is for a leader to maintain and grow relationships. It requires dealing with moving targets. This is why individual reasoning and creativity are so powerful. As leaders, we are required to run alongside them before we evaluate or criticize their actions.

LEADERSHIP UNDER CONSTRUCTION

In each statement, which response *best* describes your actual or typical leadership style:

1. When a task is assigned I . . .

a. Take action.
b. Find the best system to get it done on time.
c. Find ways to involve others.
d. Evaluate new ways of getting the job accomplished.

2. In a group of people I . . .

a. Enjoy a few deep conversations.
b. Enjoy being the center of a discussion.
c. Often become impatient with meaningless chatter.
d. Often feel uncomfortable.

3. As a member of a team I . . .

a. Value order and schedules.
b. Take charge.
c. Want everybody to feel good about working together.
d. Prefer to be delegated a specialized task I can do alone.

4. When I perceive my supervisor or boss treating me unfairly I . . .

a. Become discouraged and pessimistic.
b. Become harsh and demanding.
c. Insist on rules being followed, but won't say so.
d. Try to get others to agree with me.

5. My goal in an organization is . . .

a. Teamwork.
b. Getting promotions and raises.
c. Implementing systems that increase productivity.
d. Finding creative ways to accomplish goals.

6. When things get tense, I . . .

a. Find it hard to make decisions.
b. Don't care what others think and feel.
c. Talk to those involved to resolve the problem.
d. Resist any change.

7. When an opportunity arises, I . . .

a. Enjoy the challenge and am determined to capitalize.
b. Enjoy competition with others.
c. Need clear goals and procedures.
d. Need time to evaluate what to do.

8. When a friend is feeling down, I . . .

a. Ask questions to find out the deeper problem.
b. Am quick to give advice to fix the problem.
c. Don't know what to do.
d. Think my support can help my friend, whatever the problem is.

9. I enjoy an environment that . . .

a. Is flexible and has variety.
b. Has an organized plan to accomplish goals.
c. Lets me take action.
d. Gives me plenty of time to think and plan.

10. My thinking processes can be described as . . .

a. Logical and ordered.
b. Varied and imaginative.
c. Clear and decisive.
d. Deep and reflective.

11.   When I am in a leadership role, I . . .

a. Like to see lots of activity.
b. Like to have lots of freedom to do things my way.
c. Implement a clear system.
d. Implement a supportive team spirit.

12.   When people criticize me, I . . .

a. Try to convince them they are wrong.
b. Blow them off.
c. Consider if they are right.
d. Wilt and withdraw.

13.   I function best when I . . .

a. Can concentrate on one task at a time.
b. Get lots of positive feedback.
c. Have plenty of time to think through difficult decisions.
d. Can be in charge.

14.   In my spare time, I prefer . . .

a. To do something active.
b. To read a good book.
c. To be with friends.
d. Work on a craft or hobby.

15.   I prefer a leader who . . .

a. Is warm and supportive.
b. Challenges me to do more.
c. Provides clear expectations.
d. Allows me to communicate my opinion and feelings.

16.   When a new idea is communicated, I . . .

a. Want to know how it fits into what I am already doing.
b. Want to analyze the concept to see if it can be improved.
c. Want to make it happen.
d. Am discouraged because I didn't think of it.

17.   People would describe me as . . .

a. Intense and in charge.
b. Likable and supportive.
c. Steady as a rock.
d. Thoughtful and reflective.

18.   If I had money to invest, I would . . .

a. Carefully analyze many options before investing.
b. Value the input of a professional and do what he says.
c. Be very conservative.
d. Be willing to take great risks for the possibility of great rewards.

19.   When I am late, I . . .

a. Feel very guilty for inconveniencing others.
b. Admit it's a problem, but it doesn't matter much.
c. Blame others for the problem.
d. Develop a plan so it doesn't happen again.

20.   In a group, when someone asks for my opinion, I . . .

a. Gladly give it.
b. Defer to someone else.
c. Defy anyone to disagree with me.
d. Carefully consider my answer.

SELF-SCORING CHART

Find your responses and circle the ones that correspond with your answers:

BATTLESHIP		CRUISE SHIP	SAILBOAT	RESEARCH VESSEL
1.	A	C	D	B
2.	C	B	A	D
3.	B	C	D	A
4.	B	D	A	C
5.	D	A	B	C
6.	B	C	A	D
7.	A	B	D	C
8.	B	D	A	C
9.	C	A	D	B
10.	C	B	D	A
11.	A	D	B	C
12.	B	A	C	D
13.	D	B	C	A
14.	A	C	B	D
15.	B	A	D	C
16.	C	D	B	A
17.	A	B	D	C
18.	D	B	A	C
19.	C	B	A	D
20.	C	A	D	B
TOTALS _____		_____	_____	_____

RELATIONAL LEADERSHIP

BATTLESHIP	CRUISE SHIP	SAILBOAT	RESEARCH VESSEL
• Has a definite mission	• Doesn't necessarily plan the trip but they enjoy the ride	• Creative and enjoys trying new ways to sail	• Analytical, goal oriented and immersed in details
• Takes action	• People oriented although relationships are not always deep	• Non-confrontational, loyal, and committed to friendships	• Always follows procedures
• Asserts authority			
• Mode of operation is crisis		• Cares about people	• Flexibility is not a possibility
• Focused on power and control	• Unstructured and focused on the present	• Quiet and shy yet gives stability in times of need	• They need structure, measurable expectations, and deadlines
• Black-and-white, all-or-nothing decisions	• Great enthusiasm and very flexible and positive		
• Accepts failure as part of risk taking	• Need support and encouragement	• They're hurt deep because of their depth of reflection	• When too much is expected, it results in anger
• Relationships are based on doing something constructive	• Prefers direct communications and wants you to stick to the point	• During storms they are tossed more than other vessels	• Does not generally feel comfortable with the festive spirits
• In combat one wins, one loses	• Feelings are hurt easily	• In times of change, they need time to think and prepare	• Pride can easily result in open competition and criticism
• For smooth sailing they need clear goals, direct communications and lots of activity	• Wants lots of best friends that don't demand too much	• Articulate communicator in a safe environment	• With failure they become even more structured, a perfectionist, analytical, and critical
• Values the order, information, and effectiveness of the research vessel, but are far too slow.	• More concerned how other people will view their failure than failure itself	• Requires individualized attention	
• Becomes impatient and demanding because of the need for information.	• They need a captain	• Wants a few intimate friendships	
		• Sailboat out of control becomes withdrawn, pessimistic, and defensive	

Developing a Leadership Culture:
The Leaders New Work

CONCEPT 3.2

Accelerated change is driving the need for new ideas, which is driving the requirements for a new kind of leader.

Purpose:

Section 2 will review the characteristics of a leadership culture and review the requirements for lifelong learning.

Procedures:

- Begin with a review ("Defining Leadership Cultures" below) and a discussion of concept 3.2. Introduce lifelong learning as a key trait of learning cultures. Discuss thoroughly the conclusions reached by the class concerning lifelong learning.

- Have students read chapter 6 in *Helping Educators Lead*. After reading this chapter, students will review both "leadership performance components" and "leadership performance indicators." Using their knowledge and experience, students are to use these components and indicators to construct a model leadership culture.

- Complete activity 36 and discuss answers thoroughly.

- Review remaining material and complete activity 37.

Defining Leadership Cultures

The New Concept of a Leadership Culture:

- Everyone becomes the CEO of *ideas* by listening, searching, and thinking.

- Internal and external value is continuously created.

- Innovation is treated as duty.

- Relationship development is a requirement of the age.

- Leaders become masters of paradox and understanding. They learn to cope with reality and ambiguity as well as understand new situations (environments) that continually emerge from constant change.

- People learn how to let go.

- People embrace an organizational life of temporary work groups, resulting in feelings of uprootedness and unconnectedness.

- Ongoing learning and thinking dominate leadership cultures where power is based on the effectiveness of collaboration and reason.

REMEMBER: LEADERSHIP CULTURES INVEST IN LIFELONG LEARNING

Characteristics of Learning Organizations

Learning Organizations Maintain the Joy of Learning	Learning Organizations Understand That Superior Performance Depends upon Superior Learning	Learning Organizations Are Committed to Problem-Solving and Problem-Finding
• We are designed for learning. • We are born with a curiosity to learn. • We can continue to find joy in learning.	• Increasingly, the key to survival is the creation of new wealth for both the individual and the corporation. • Top-down thinking gives way to integrated thinking and acting at all levels. • The collective genius and actions of people are harvested at all levels. • An evolution of learning is about creating rather than maintaining.	• Ideas and information come through unhampered. • Problem-solvers know how to seek out the different and the unusual. • Problem-seekers are perhaps the most flexible and knowledgeable people in the organization.

It needs to be pointed out that continuing education will become a distinctive characteristic of the 21st century because of the rate of professional obsolescence.

Activity 36: Lifelong Learning

Directions: In the spaces below, describe your *ideal* organization and the way it promotes lifelong learning. Then, describe how you would promote lifelong learning in your organization.

Ideal Organization

_____

_____

_____

_____

Ways you would promote lifelong learning

1. _____

_____

_____

2. _____

_____

_____

3. _____

_____

_____

4. _____

_____

_____

5. _____

_____

_____

LEADERSHIP CULTURES CREATE AND
MAINTAIN ENTREPRENEURIAL ENVIRONMENTS

What an entrepreneurial environment is not:

- Rules have replaced informality.

- Claiming turf has replaced teamwork.

- E-mail/V-mail have replaced face-to-face communication.

- Supervisory layers have replaced impromptu visits.

- Traditions, traditional thinkers, and bureaucrats prevent getting the job done.

What an entrepreneurial environment is:

- Motivated by a cause in which they believe; surrounded by associates they respect; and convinced they will not be defeated.

- Trust is generated and provides hope, meaning, direction, and success.

- New ideas are encouraged and accepted.

- Work is one project followed by another project resulting in small wins.

- Organizations are temporary work groups of diverse specialists.

What an entrepreneurial leader demands:

- That employees deliver more than expected.

- That results are the reward.

- That flexible groups and networks create each other.

- That no one is as smart as everyone.

- That individual satisfactions will increase.

- That adaptive, diverse, problem-solvers are linked by a need to insure customer value.

Learning disabilities are tragic in children, but they are fatal in organizations. Because of them, few organizations live half the average life span as a person.—Peter Senge, 1990

LEADERSHIP CULTURES CREATE PROMOTE SERVICE AS THE LIFE-STYLE OF THE ORGANIZATION

Principles:

- All organizations are service organizations to the degree that they create value for customers through performance.

- Nothing is more important to a service culture's success than to establish and instill confidence in customers that it can and will keep its promises.

- Sustaining customer confidence is dependent on those inside and outside the organization that create customer value.

The most common service needs from leaders within leadership cultures:

SERVICE NEEDS:	LEADERS PROVIDE:
Direction and meaning	Vision and purpose
Trust	Integrity and authority
Hope	Optimism
Belonging	Community
Involvement	Empowerment
Results	Bias toward action

From Warren Bennis, 1999

Success:

Success will be sustained in a service/leadership culture in the following ways:

- Act entrepreneurial so your clientele will discover how easy it is to do business with you, and your employees will discover how flexible and innovative they can become.

- Establish organizational values that inspire and guide your service providers.

- Maintain a strategic focus that is driven by constancy of purpose.

- Build trust-based relationships, for these will be the measure of your future.

- Continually raise the service delivery standard.

- Employ those whose personal values will support and sustain organizational values.

- Make your image a reinforcing performer of service.

- Be a giving company. Selfishness turns people and organizations inward and prevents them from serving their clientele.

- Invest in the success of people.

If you believe performance quality is the key to an organization's future; if you believe strong employee relationships enable performance quality; if you believe you are hiring great people, then to invest in their success is a logical outcome of your beliefs.—H. Darrell Young

Leadership Cultures Require Focused Competencies from Leaders

- Leaders should possess the capacity to manage and control change. Here the leader becomes a *designer*, planning, conceiving ideas, developing a purpose, and executing a plan.

- Leaders should also possess the capacity to manage their behaviors, becoming *stewards* of the organization. Stewardship requires the know-how and responsibility to efficiently manage the assets of the organization.

- Finally, leaders should be *teachers,* imparting what has been learned to others and nurturing their growth.

Activity 37: Gaining Understanding

Directions: Study the behavior characteristics in the right-hand column. In groups of two or three, choose characteristics from the right-hand column that define the three leadership modalities in the left-hand column. Be prepared to justify your choices in a classroom discussion.

Designer

_____ • Consistent, yet flexible.

_____ • Ownership for those who they lead and
                                           the skills they promote to increase value.

_____ • Unites people.

_____ • Communicates a consistent message.

_____ • Bias toward action.

Teacher

_____ • Insures hope and belonging.

_____ • Develops direction and meaning.

_____ • Creates effective learning processes.

_____ • Begins the process of renewal.

_____ • Builds trust-based relationships.

_____ • Includes employees in decisions and
                                           change.

Steward

_____ • Fosters strategic thinking.

_____ • Expands capabilities of employees

                                           through evaluation (measurements).

_____ • Empowers, enables, and serves others.

_____ • Encourages new ideas.

_____ • Freely becomes a mentor for others.

_____ • Encourages networking and leading by
                                           knowledge rather than by position.

_____

THINGS TO REMEMBER

- Ordinary people can do extraordinary things; they can learn to lead.

- Leadership cultures maintain the joy of learning.

- Leaders are stewards of the disciplines of a learning organization.

- A key competitive advantage is to create a lifelong learning environment that is adaptive.

- Leadership cultures promote entrepreneurial environments with an organizational commitment to a lifestyle of service.

- Leaders are service providers.

- Success in the 21st century will be determined largely by our ability to manage change, manage ourselves, and serve others.

- The objective of great leadership models is not to establish an institution so much as to show us a life worth living.

CONCEPT 3.3
Leaders are made great by their followers and followers are made great by their leaders.

Purpose:

The purpose of this section is to increase student understanding of "followship" as a prerequisite for effective leadership.

Procedures:

- With students, discuss concept 3.3. Find out what they think it means and list their various interpretations where all can see.

- Follow with a discussion of the case study of Abraham Lincoln. When completed, return to concept 3.3 and the students' interpretations. Ask if anyone would like to change his or her interpretation or amend it in any way.

- Conclude with "Things to Remember."

CASE STUDY: ABRAHAM LINCOLN

(The following is adapted from *Lincoln on Leadership* by Donald T. Philips.)

Effective leadership can best be understood by examining the lives of individuals like Abraham Lincoln who have demonstrated leadership mastery under sometimes harsh and extreme conditions. Lincoln was President of the United States during one of our country's most critical times, yet his experience was meager: he had never before held an executive position; he had only served in Congress for one term; and he had no military experience of significance, he had never been in battle.

But, Lincoln was one of our country's greatest leaders. The foundation of his leadership style was a commitment to the rights of the individual, a commitment to principle, and continuous study. Although he grew up in poverty, Lincoln studied history, the Bible, and the law. He had a binding link to common people and stood for what was right, honest, and self-evident.

From Lincoln's model of effective leadership we learn the following:

1. HE ACQUIRED NEW SKILLS FROM HIS FOLLOWERS AND WAS COMMITTED TO LEARNING WHILE ON THE JOB.

Evidence of this comes from his spending time with his troops, his need to be accessible to everyone, his preference for relaxed environments for personal dialogue, and his ability to personally collect information that he needed for decision making.

2. HE BELIEVED HUMAN ACTIONS CAN BE JUSTIFIED, BUT HUMAN NATURE CAN'T BE CHANGED.

We find that he built strong alliances both personally and professionally. He let the individuals in these alliances know that he was firm in his commitment to duty. Within these alliances he discovered that trust is learned by example, how his people responded to situations, and who shared his ethics and values.

3. HE WON FOLLOWERS TO HIS CAUSE BY MAKING THEM HIS FRIENDS.

Lincoln used persuasion rather than coercion, for he knew the value of making a request rather than merely giving an order. For example, to McClellan he said, "This letter is in no sense an order." To Halleck he responded, "I hope you will consider it." Finally, to Grant he said, "If there is anything wanting which is in my power to give, do not fail to let me know." Lincoln teaches us that it is more effective to seek consent from followers in order to lead them, and that if you practice dictatorship, you will soon be on a dictator's receiving end.

4. HE BELIEVED THAT IF YOU FORFEIT THE CONFIDENCE OF YOUR FOLLOWERS, YOU CAN NEVER REGAIN THEIR RESPECT AND ESTEEM.

We learn from Lincoln that honesty and integrity are the building blocks of leadership and that divorced from ethics, leadership is reduced to mere technique.

5. HE TAUGHT US NEVER TO ACT OUT OF VENGEANCE OR SPITE BECAUSE ONCE WE DESTROY A FOLLOWER, HE OR SHE CEASES TO CONTRIBUTE TO THE ORGANIZATION.

At the end of the Civil War, Lincoln requested that Dixie be played at a rally outside the White House. This strong statement let others know that he would not seek revenge now that the war was over. We learn the important maxim that we should never step on a person when he is down, for this will make him and his friends enemies of the organization.

CONSIDER: Edwin M. Stanton, Secretary of War during Lincoln's presidency, once said about Lincoln that the President had "no token of any intelligent understanding." Even with this, Lincoln appointed Stanton because he knew he was the best man for the job. When Lincoln died it was Stanton who commented, "Now he belongs to the ages." The President's son Robert recalled that for more than ten days after his father's death, Stanton would come by his room and spend the first few minutes of his visit weeping without saying a word.

6. HE TAUGHT US THAT GREAT LEADERS WOULD ENCOUNTER SLANDER BY VIRTUE OF THE POSITION HELD.

From him we know that how we let it affect us reveals the strength or weakness of our character. This is the difference. Hemingway's definition of courage was "Maintain grace under pressure." Lincoln was slandered, libeled, and hated perhaps more intensely than any man ever to run for the presidency. As a result of his election, the South seceded, the Civil War was fought, and during the war criticism of Lincoln reached maximum proportions. He was publicly called every name imaginable by the press including a grotesque baboon, third rate country lawyer who split rails and split the union, a coarse vulgar joker, a dictator, an ape, a buffoon, and many more. The *Illinois State Register* labeled him the craftiest and most dishonest politician that ever disgraced an office in America. It did not subside after he took office; it then came from Congress, the Republican Party, his cabinet, and his generals.

7. HE TAUGHT US HOW TO BE A MASTER OF PARADOX.

Paradox is probably the most appropriate description for not only Lincoln the man, but also Lincoln the leader. He was consistent, yet flexible. He treated people, from all walks of life, with respect and dignity. He once said, "My policy is to have no policy, always leave an opportunity for a change of mind." Lincoln was also charismatic, yet unassuming. Although he was a victim of slander and malice, he was immensely popular with his troops. He was patient, yet calculating. Lincoln had a revolving door of generals whom he often removed and replaced, yet in reality, he gave them ample time and support to produce results. From him we learn the following:

- Remain flexible without being relativistic.

- Convince others without being rigid.

- Be willing to control situations without being offensive.

- Learn to be gentle without being soft.

- Be convincing without being manipulative.

8. FROM LINCOLN WE LEARN THAT PERSONAL WARS WILL NOT BE WON BY STRATEGY ALONE; HARD WORK IS REQUIRED.

Although leaders take charge, make decisions, and assure results, Lincoln was a servant of the people and, as such, they had the right to know why he made his decisions.

9. HE TAUGHT US THAT WE SHOULD LET PEOPLE KNOW THAT THE HONOR WILL BE ALL THEIRS IF THEY SUCCEED, AND THE BLAME HIS [THE LEADER] IF THEY FAIL.

If we fail to honor people, they will fail to honor us. Lead by being led and listen to people and talk with them a little. Be guided by what you hear without being threatened. Give them credit when it is due and make sure mistakes are ours, not theirs. Be in control; stay informed to assure that their ideas and actions match the purposes of the organization. Help individuals work out their differences by bringing them together for counsel and dialogue.

10. HE KEPT SEARCHING UNTIL HE FOUND HIS GRANT AND SO SHOULD WE.

Lincoln launched a three-year search for a general who would get the job done. He wanted a general who would crave responsibility, take risks, and most importantly, make things happen. Lincoln's search took him through the following men:

Truin C. McDowell was a commanding general overwhelmed by responsibility and, therefore, hesitated to act. Instead of taking action, he chose to build up and train his forces. At Bull Run, the first major offensive of the war, McDowell argued for more time to prepare. After four months, Lincoln decided he was not the man for the job.

John C. Fremont was a general in the Department of the West. Lincoln said of Fremont, "His cardinal mistake is that he isolates himself and allows nobody to see him, and by which he does not know what is going on in the very matter he is dealing with."

George B. McClellan was general-in-chief and a man of impeccable credentials and reputation. No one was better for the job of staffing, training, and administering the disorganized and defeated troops from the battle of Bull Run. In the long run, his negative side overshadowed his qualities. He overanalyzed and remained inactive. He simply would not fight. He continually delayed by asking for more troops because he always feared being outnumbered. McClellan would not act. Lincoln said, "He has the slows." He was overcautious and lacked the decisiveness to take the offensive. A victory, he thought, was defending his ground. He was demoted after four and a half months.

Henry W. Halleck was also general-in-chief and once worked for McClellan. Lincoln gave him the authority to fire McClellan if necessary. He did not. He was a West Point graduate and had written a book on military strategy. After a second defeat at Bull Run, Halleck blamed himself for the loss and refused to act thereafter. After the battle, he began to evade all responsibility. He lasted three and a half months before he was made a figurehead, which allowed him to keep his title.

John A. McClernand of the Department of the Mississippi was aggressive, but a poor general. He was territorial, overly ambitious, and wanted all credit for himself. He was a habitual complainer about his colleagues. He lasted three months before he was placed under Grant, one of the colleagues he attacked.

Ambrose E. Burnside served in the Department of the Potomac but was not competent enough to command such a large army. He lasted only two and a half months. After losing a battle with 12,000 casualties, he broke down and lost all control. His subordinates began to question his ability. Burnside went to the President to ask for their dismissal, but instead, the President dismissed Burnside.

Nathaniel P. Banks in the Department of the Gulf took action only when prodded by the President. He always needed more men and supplies. Eventually, Lincoln sent him to oversee reconstruction in Louisiana.

Joseph Hooker was in the Department of the Potomac and took over the army in the winter months. He had the perfect excuse for inactivity—inclement weather. He was overconfident, but subordinate officers continued to complain about him. Lincoln confronted him about this and asked him to get his problems worked out. Hooker lasted five months when Lincoln replaced him with George Meade—one of Hooker's chief antagonists.

George C. Meade of the Department of the Potomac immediately mobilized the army and bravely and skillfully directed his troops for a three-day battle and victory at Gettysburg. Lincoln realized that the war could come to an end if Meade would mount an offensive and crush the severely wounded Confederate Army of Northern Virginia, but Meade did not follow through, being satisfied with his victory at Gettysburg. Cautious hesitation caused Lincoln to become visibly upset with Meade. He felt Meade was better suited for taking than giving orders and replaced him with Ulysses S. Grant.

Ulysses S. Grant became general-in-chief and Lincoln found that he could effectively give Grant a free hand to run the war. Grant had all the characteristics the others did not have, and he didn't have to spend an inordinate amount of time overseeing his work. However, Lincoln never relinquished total control of authority. He monitored and exerted influence when he felt it was necessary.

11. HE TAUGHT US NOT TO LOSE CONFIDENCE IN OUR ASSOCIATES WHEN THEY FAIL.

Lincoln had great tolerance for failure because he knew if his generals were not making mistakes, they were not moving. He viewed the failures of his generals as *learning events;* thus, he always encouraged innovation. He stood by his commanders, giving them encouragement. He also found that the best leaders never stopped learning. They have the capacity to be taught by whomever they come in contact.

12. WE LEARN FROM HIM THAT "AN INTELLIGENT COMMUNICATOR" IS CAREFUL ABOUT WHAT, WHO, AND WHEN HE OR SHE SAYS SOMETHING.

Lincoln was clear and confident in what he had to say and followed through with his own actions. He understood that there are times when one should not speak; to not make mistakes publicly. When a leader speaks, everything is intently heard; therefore, when a leader makes a mistake publicly, it affects both the leader and the entire organization. A good idea is to couple written documents with verbal discussions, thereby catching the idea with two different forms of communication. Using one's ability to see and read as well as listen and speak will increase the memory power of the entire organization.

13. THE SINGLE MOST EFFECTIVE (AND IMPORTANT) DIMENSION OF LINCOLN'S LEADERSHIP STYLE WAS INFLUENCING PEOPLE THROUGH CONVERSATION AND STORYTELLING.

Lincoln used storytelling for a purpose rather than amusement. It had the power to awaken his followers because effective communication had motivational strength and usually contained humor, which was a major force in his ability to persuade people. *Remember: loyalty is more often won through private conversation than in any other way.*

14. HE KEPT REMINDING HIS PEOPLE OF THE BASIC PRINCIPLES UPON WHICH OUR NATION WAS FOUNDED.

A leader's responsibility is to reassert, remind, and affirm the basic principles of his or her organization at every conceivable opportunity. A leader should verbally affirm a vision and continually reaffirm it. Effective visions cannot be forced on the masses. It is the responsibility of the leader to set them in motion by calling on the past, relating it to the present, and linking both to a desired outcome in the future.

15. HE LEFT A LEGACY.

How would you like your leadership legacy to read? Horace Greeley, a newspaper man, had this to say about Lincoln after Lincoln's death:

He slowly won his way to eminence and fame by doing the work that lay next to him—doing it with all his growing might—doing it as well as he could, and learning by his failure, when failure was encountered, how to do it better. . . . He was open to all impressions and influences, and gladly profited by the teachings of events and circumstances, no matter how adverse or unwelcome. There was probably no year of his life when he was not wiser, cooler, and a better man than he had been the year proceeding.—Lincoln on Leadership by Donald T. Philips

Activity 38: Lifelong Learning

Directions: In the spaces below list what you believe are the five characteristics that made Lincoln one of our nation's greatest leaders. Be prepared to discuss these beliefs in small groups and then share with the class. The class will make a composite list of these characteristics.

1.

2.

3.

4.

5.

THINGS TO REMEMBER

- Great leaders recognize that the big rewards come to those who are willing to go the extra mile.

- Great leaders are always accessible to everyone.

- Great leaders are unpredictable; they have no routine.

- Great leaders sense an objection before it advances and they generate questions from the questions of others.

- Great leaders seldom argue and they never fight a battle where nothing is gained by winning.

- Great leaders provide great service and, as such, they regenerate themselves as great leaders.

- A great leadership model is one whose energies are challenged by the promise of obstacles rather than the picture of rewards.

Divesting Self and Investing in Others

CONCEPT 3.4

As we grow as people, we grow in relationships; as we grow in relationships, we grow as people. As we grow in both we will have earned the right to be called "leader."

TO THE TEACHER

Purpose:

The purpose of this section is to review the foundations for building ethical relationships in businesses, schools, and other organizations.

Procedures:

- Thoroughly discuss concept 3.4 with the class.

- Go over the material in this section (in detail).

- Complete activities 39, 40, 41, and 42.

- Conclude with Summary and Things to Remember.

BUILDING COVENANTAL PARTNERSHIPS

How is a business or other organization to be organized? Many will think in terms of departments, teams, and a leadership pyramid, but effective leaders will first think about the organization's moral foundations. This will entail such considerations as the following:

- What will its ethical code include?

- How are relationships built on the inside of the organization and between the organization and its clients?

- How can a leadership culture be created and maintained throughout the organization?

- How can we create and maintain covenantal partnerships?

In this final section, we examine these questions, focusing on the moral premises that sustain the life and quality of organizations and businesses. These premises highlight the organization's interest in moral integration and social responsibility as a means of serving its clients. This idea—of serving—will flow from the top to the bottom of the organization and from the organization outward to its clients. "Service" is the behavior that permeates covenantal partnerships and sustains their life.

In section 3, the concept of "covenant" is the framework around which "divesting self and investing in others" is built. Shared partnerships are covenantal partnerships. In his book, *Leadership Is an Art*, Max Dupree makes the following insightful observation: *Covenantal partnerships induce freedom, rest on shared commitment to ideas, to issues, to values, to goals, to management process. Covenantal partnerships are open to influence, they fill deep needs, and they work to have meaning and be fulfilling. They reflect unity, grace, and praise, they are hospitable to the unusual person and unusual ideas, and they tolerate risk and forgive errors.*

What we need to remember about the theory of covenant is that it is a theory of moral ordering; at the same time, it speaks to the nature of consent and the limits of authority. The covenant idea comes to us from Hebraic and Christian sources. In biblical history, the interaction of God and humankind is marked by a series of covenants or treaties. Within covenant, God *promises* salvation through divine grace. The *condition* of such an agreement is faith and obedience. Thus, there is a conditional element here, and with it, mutual *obligations*. As a result, although God's sovereignty is complete, the human perception of its nature is transformed. Although man and God are not equal, in covenant, they become *responsible* to each other. Covenant creates *expectations* that God will act reasonably and with justice. Thus, humankind is able to accept subordination with dignity and without being debased, degraded, or enslaved.

The compact creates a self-conscious moral order. Humans agree to uphold a code of responsible conduct by fulfilling obligations to family and community and God agrees to uphold his promise of eternal life. These commitments are both personal and communal, creating social norms and a moral ordering. Unlike a contract, covenant suggests an indefeasible commitment and a continuing relationship. This covenant bond is relatively *unconditional and indissoluble*. It is *open-ended* and implicates the whole person, the group, or the organization in its moral ordering and obligations.

We find in covenant a commitment to foundational principles, to beliefs and resolves that define the moral premises of a practice, association, or community. Contracts bind individuals to explicit and limited terms. Covenants are more ambiguous: *obligations are not fully specified in advance; the covenantal promise is a beginning, not an end; and obligations derive from the nature of the relationships and are not founded in consent nor created through negotiation.* The moral foundation of a covenant includes the following:

- Personal freedom and judgment

- Obligations to control and correct personal desires

- Concern for the well-being of others

- Acknowledgement of the importance of history and the desire to leave a moral legacy

- Corrosion and deterioration, improvement and creativity because we are all human

- A vibrant and active morality that is fully conscious of the lives of people

The American Declaration of Independence is properly thought of as a covenantal foundation for the United States Constitution. It contains a ringing affirmation of moral and political principles, which are the touchstones of . . .

- Constitutional *formation* (the moral principles embedded in law),

- Constitutional *validity* (law is itself evaluated or judged by moral principles), and

- Constitutional *growth* (like humans, law changes with time but must remain morally consistent).

Abraham Lincoln's conception of a national covenant has been summarized by John Schaar in the following words:

> *We are a nation formed by a covenant, by dedication to a set of principles and by an exchange of promises to uphold and advance certain commitments among ourselves and throughout the world. Those principles and commitments are the core of American identity, the soul of the body politic. They make the American nation unique, and uniquely valuable, among and to the other nations. But the other side of the conception contains a warning very much like the warning spoken by the prophets of Israel: if we fail in our promises to each other, and lose the principles of the covenant, then we lose everything, for they are we.*—John Schaar, *Legitimacy and the Modern State*

METHODS FOR BUILDING COVENANTAL PARTNERSHIPS

1. **A covenant connotes shared values, beliefs, and vision.** The leader's responsibility is to paint a picture of the future with a mixture of realism and optimism, preparing the organization for future possibilities. Remember: promise only what you can— your friendship and companionship. The leader does not have to predict the future, only call for mutual trust and faith in his or her vision. If your organization is to become a moral community, then its chief covenantal premise is that all persons are equal; each has equal moral competence where everybody is to count for one and nobody for more than one.

2. **A covenant relationship is a time-sharing relationship.** Every leader should understand that to empower a person means to provide opportunities for that person to become fully realized. Given time, everyone can form a self; can invest that self with intrinsic worth; can make it the embodiment of personal and social continuity; can exhibit concern for self-respect and self-determination; and can reach out to others for sympathy and in sympathy. To empower means to spend time with—followers must have access to leaders if they are to become the leader's priority.

Empowerment is build around a push-and-pull relationship. Leaders may think they are pulling their followers along; whereas followers may think they have to push their leaders in the direction of sustained discovery and success. Both are true and this strikes at the heart of a true covenantal relationship: as a leader, I am pushing my vision on you and pulling you along with it. On the other hand, as a follower, who is truly interacting in a positive manner within the covenantal relationship, I am also pushing my ideas on the leader and pulling the leader in my direction. This is the essence of sustained dialogue: openness, understanding, and mutual respect.

3. **Shared learning focuses on the covenant of reason.** This is what John Dewey called "the method of intelligence." By this he meant a commitment to shared discovery—by rational inquiry, including learning from experience—of what is good to have and right to do. It is the leader's responsibility to be a perpetual learner and to create an environment where learning happens. This means supporting innovative learning (discovery) and learning that is future-oriented and challenges the undoing of bad habits and empty traditions. Problem solving is a part of this learning cycle. Organizations thrive in problem solving and challenge-oriented environments. Maintenance learning that deals with known and recurring situations will enhance our problem solving abilities as we gain understanding of the patterns associated with our personal and organizational activities.

One cannot afford to hoard human resources. People either grow or turn rancid and sour. They can't be put on the shelf.—Peter Drucker

4. **Leaders, to be leaders, are risk takers.** Leaders should share their risks with others. The challenge is to enlarge accountability without giving up the main benefit of autonomy: long-range, flexible, purposive, nonpolitical (moral) leadership. Effective leaders allow their followers to fail, for they too have failed. They are not looking for perfection, but faith in a vision.

For a lot of people, the word failure carries with it a finality, but for the successful leader, failure is a beginning . . . the springboard of hope.—Warren Bennis

Activity 39: Provide Examples

Directions: In the space below, provide examples from your personal experiences of the four methods of building covenantal partnerships:

1.

_____

_____

_____

_____

2.

_____

_____

_____

_____

3.

_____

_____

_____

_____

4.

_____

_____

_____

_____

LOVE (LOYALTY, COMMITMENT, AND FIDELITY) IS

THE FOUNDATION FOR DIVESTING AND INVESTING IN OTHERS

The best kept secret of leaders is love. Leadership is an affair of the heart. Not of the head. Of all things that sustain a leader, love is most lasting.—Warren Bennis

Only a context of commitment in which the unique person matters generates full concern for the well-being of others. Morality is not disinterested in people. It is magnificently other-regarding. Morality proliferates in human importance because of the importance of human relationships, even when the dominant themes of our culture wrap people up in egotistical things instead of looking at deeper meanings. When people matter, we are compelled to recognize the primacy of love over justice, over rationality, and over any other method of decision making and problem solving. One thing we learn from our religious faith is that we cannot love without caring for specific persons for their own sake; that is, we are called upon to love "the neighbor," not mankind or the human race. Love requires that in our day-to-day activities we detect the neighbor underneath the deals and the competition and the special interests.

One of the surest signs of leadership greatness is to be above personal resentment and small annoyances. Pettiness always brings its own reward. Implicit in servant and ethical leadership are deep metaphors embedded in our principles and overtly shared in our behaviors. We cannot avoid the ethical horizon that servant leadership begs for us to attend. All around us, everyday, we are bombarded by cultures that draw our attention and give us meaning. The *culture of detachment* sees the world as basically hostile and humans as largely self-absorbed with only small amounts of energy for larger, altruistic ventures. This detachment-based culture oscillates between ethical egoism ("me first, you not at all") and cautious reciprocity ("me first, you second, maybe"). The *culture of joy* reminds us that the world is fundamentally harmonious and that relationships are important to sustaining our vision. The *culture of control* sees humans primarily as contolled and controllable. Leaders who follow this culture are as much controlled (with intimidation and force) by their environments as they try to control them. The *culture of care*, on the other hand, understands the tensions and anxieties of life and gravitates toward an ethic that finds a place for both self-love and self-transcending love for the other. The deep metaphors we find in the ethic of care remind us of the human ideal of fulfillment and the sometimes necessity of self-sacrifice. Divesting of self is a self-emptying or self-offering that lies at the heart of civility and the creation of social capital. Divesting of self and investing in others are the fibers out of which true community is fashioned. This is more than a matter of taste or personal choice, it goes to the heart of our character. It is a matter of our vision of how society should be constructed and how people should relate to one another—matters that cannot be arbitrated in contracts or business agreements.

Where teamwork is a priority, groups composed of people who prioritize the more humanistic values (the cultures of joy and care)—cooperation, self-acceptance, and community service—speed ahead. It has been shown that by cooperating with their own kind, groups of cooperators compete better against other groups, espeically groups that try to exploit others. Quite the opposite, by competing with their own kind, groups of competitors—those who value individual materialistic advancement, attractiveness, and fame—compete much worse against other groups. (Giacomo Bono and Michael E. McCullough, *Research on Other-Regarding Virtues,* 1998–2003, in Stephen G. Post et al., *Research on Altruism and Love,* Philadelphia: Templeton Foundation, 2003).

Great leaders do their work and move on. They cannot afford the cultures of detachment and control. They let each experience—negative and positive—penetrate them fully. That's how they are able to leave and move on. We learn from Lincoln, as well as from other great men and women, that positive growth is built from respect, ethical values, communication, the ability to compromise, and forgiveness. Years ago a messenger left the White House with a message to Secretary Stanton from President Lincoln. Upon his return, the messenger was asked if he had delivered the message. Angrily, the messenger replied, "Yes." Mr. Lincoln asked, "What was Stanton's reply?" "He tore it up. And what's more, he said you are a fool!" Lincoln's reply was, "Well, I reckon its true, because Stanton is usually right."

Albert Schweitzer once said, "The only possible way out of chaos is for us to come once more under the control of the ideas of true civilization through the adoption of an attitude toward life that contains those ideas. But what is the nature of the attitude toward life in which the will to general progress and to ethical progress are alike founded and in which they are bound together? It consists in an ethical affirmation of the world and life" (*Reverence for Life*, New York: Philosophical Library, 1965).

METHODS OF DIVESTING AND INVESTING
IN ORDER TO GROW OTHERS

EMPOWERING
To Give Power or Authority

We have seen that managing suggests a rational, efficient-minded, goal-oriented organization. This is the realm of administration, not leadership. When we manage, ends are taken as given, and every act is justified by the contribution it makes to those ends. All else is distraction. Managerial authority depends on what has been called "the zone of indifference" (Chester I. Barnard, *The Function of the Executive*). In this zone, employees, students, and soldiers are expected to defer to legitimate authority, having agreed beforehand to subordinate their own preferences and suspend their own judgments within well-defined limits.

We know that this well-ordered world of management by authority, deference, and limited commitment is not easily maintained. To lead is to accept responsibility *for the whole of the organization*. It means investing power and authority in others. This is quite different from the rational coordination of specialized activities. Leadership takes account of all the interests that affect the viability, competence, and moral character of the organization. By position, by influence, and in the service to others (rather than to self) leaders win the cooperation of followers more solidly by divesting themselves of some authority and investing in others through training and incentives.

The key to empowerment is belief in the abilities of the people who work in the organization. A fact that needs to be pointed out is that only secure leaders give power to others and only empowered people can reach their potential. Empowerment encourages freedom and creativity, the cost of which can be high. But when things go wrong, great leaders don't blame others; blaming others is a protective tactic in which personal responsibility is denied. Returning to Abraham Lincoln for a moment, a careful examination of his leadership style shows that his own personal security allowed him to obtain authority by giving it to others, and by accepting public responsibility for battles lost or opportunities missed.

Empowering others gets work completed more efficiently and assists in turning followers into leaders. Empowerment is growth-oriented and is based on the principle of improving each person in the organization as a way of improving the organization itself. Empowering others means an unending faith in them. It also means giving them the freedom to fail and the faith to reinstate them. This kind of leadership depends a lot on patience and self-control. It does not mean giving up responsibility or accountability for the work of the organization. Rather, it means sharing these with those whose task it is to plan, develop, and carry out the goals of the organization.

Leaders many times are afraid to empower others because they feel they cannot make others indispensible. The truth is, the only way to make yourself indispensible is to become dispensable or not necessary. Likewise, those who resist change shun empowering others because empowerment means constant change as it encourages growth in the empowered and creative activity. Some managers do not have the self-esteem, personal values, or self-worth to entrust decision making in the hands of others. As they have gained their own self-worth from their upward movement through the organization, they feel that giving back or giving up authority and power to subordinates degrades and belittles what they have accomplished (their successes and their position in the organization).

In summary, *empowerment* requires the following:

- Respect for all individuals within the organization, recognizing both their potential and hidden abilities.

- Measurement and confrontation to insure growth.

- Honest, flexible, and disciplined leaders and followers.

- Entrusting people with bigger and bigger tasks, thereby growing people and the organization.

- A significant time investment in people.

- Telling people they are important to the success of the organization.

- Assuring increased productivity because people feel they make a difference to the organization.

ENABLING
To Make Possible;
To Eliminate Roadblocks

At the heart of everything I've done has been the thought of enabling others, getting the roadblocks out of the way, out of their thinking and their systems, to enable them to become all that they can be.—Peter Drucker

Drucker's Maxims

Learning by doing: Don't put people just in learning experiences, put them in doing. Achieving enables them to grow.

Staying with someone: If someone is willing to try hard, you have an obligation to help; but if they are unwilling to try, you are under no obligation.

The teacher/disciple mix: No one is able to develop everyone. The mark of a good teacher is knowing whom he/she can develop and whom he.she cannot.

Choosing models: Don't push your people to work with other people who are not good models.

Expect problems: All you know when you choose someone is that they will bring problems. The rest you hope for.

Requirements for Enabling Others to Act

1. **Eliminating barriers** that include self-interest, worrying about who gets the credit for a job well done, and an exclusive focus on "my" work rather than on the work of the people we serve and the whole organization.

2. **Fostering collaboration** by creating cooperative goals that build trust and promote reliance and that elimate internal competition. We need to understand that individuals and departments cannot accomplish alone what the whole organization can accomplish working together. Collaboration allows us to learn more and to gain different perspectives from others. Collaboration enables us to accomplish work that we could not do effectively by ourselves.

3. **Developing cooperation** throughout the organization. People are successful when others succeed. The benefits of cooperation are long-lasting and of deep personal value. On the other hand, in competition people usually reach their goals when others perform ineffectively or fail, therefore, they are tempted to mislead and not give assistance. In competition people won't trust others for fear of being exploited, which results in frustration,

hostility, and low productivity. In competition, short-term gains generally outweigh long-term benefits.

4. Enabling others by strengthening others teaches us the following . . .

- **Trust** by making ourselves vulnerable to others whose subsequent behavior we cannot control.

- **Encouragement** or a sense of covenant. When we want someone to do something for us, we must first demonstrate our willingness to help them. This creates a personal bond that goes beyond the immediate job or one's position in the organization.

- **How to recognize** that people have real and perceived value, that their work is critical to the success of the organization.

SERVING

To Do What Is Needed;
To Honor and Obey

You can tell how you're doing as a servant by how you react when you are treated as one.
—Gordon McDonald

WHAT SERVING PEOPLE IS NOT	**WHAT SERVING PEOPLE IS**
• Giving up your personhood • Weakness • Abdication • Letting your service become more important than those whom you are serving.	• Being secure in your destiny • Having a strong self-image • Taking responsibility • Acknowledging that people are our greatest asset and they have human needs and weaknesses like you.

WHAT SERVING PEOPLE REQUIRES

- That we accept people as they are, not as we would like them to be.

- That we approach relationships and problems in terms of the present rather than the past.

- That we treat those who are close to us with the same courteous attention we extend to strangers and casual acquaintances.

- That we trust others even if the risk seems to be great.

- That we honor people through recognition and celebrate what we value.

COACHING

Linking Influence to Relationships

Concepts like "covenantal partnerships," "empowerment," "enabling," and "serving" have little value as words unless we embrace their meanings and reinforce them with our actions. By our behavior we begin to experience the meaning of ethical leadership and the "what is in it for me" value that ethical leadership brings us. We have emphasized the point throughout these three workbooks that leadership development is a continuous process and takes dedication, commitment, time, and diligence to become effective. Leadership development is not for the mentally or physically lazy; neither is it for those who only desire *position power*.

Our trek toward developing our leadership abilities will also require continuous self-evaluation, overall organization evaluation, and evaluations performed from outside sources. Evaluation ensures improvement and growth. It keeps us focused on the purposes and goals with which we have been charged. It is always possible to strengthen our leadership capability. Even effective leaders agree that continuous improvement is a necessity in a volatile world. Continuous improvement is the link between leadership development, management performance, and increasing organizational and shareholder value.

All leaders need coaches and all leaders need to become coaches within their organization. Leaders must teach the next generation of leaders. The leadership payoff frames the organization's return on investment. Leadership development will bring new knowledge, new practices, and new thinking to the challenges of the day. Leadership coaching will make sure new skills are applied in the workplace. Knowledge, new skills, and building an external and internal coaching network add up to increased personal and organizational capability.

The following exercise will help us understand the importance of leadership coaching. Remember: external training programs and leadership coaching add value to the organization only to the extent that they are applicable to the company's needs. Objectives should be clear and measurements real. Any coaching program should be aligned with the specific needs of the organization.

Activity 40: Leadership Coaching

Directions: Listed below are some of the many things coaches do for their players. Read these carefully, then list in order of priority what leadership coaching characteristics you would most value in someone else, and what leadership coaching characteristics you feel others would most value in you (Activity influenced by *The Next Generation Leader,* Andy Stanley, 2003).

LEADERSHIP COACHING CHARACTERISTICS

Coaches . . .

1. Help assess the present to ensure a more productive and effective future.

2. Advise when needed, not just when asked.

3. Observe and evaluate in many different settings.

4. Teach and instruct. Leadership coaches understand that if students are not teachable, they are not coachable.

5. Articulate their thoughts with clarity and precision.

6. Understand that what they see counts for more than what they know.

7. Operate behind the scenes.

8. Are inspirational and instill in you a mental image of who you are and what you are capable of doing.

9. Help develop performance standards and benchmarks to make certain that performance is being evaluated relative to your strengths, rather than to another person's strengths.

10. Know your capabilities and push you to your limits, which helps close the gap between potential and performance.

11. Focus is not problem solving; leadership coaches are stakeholders (investors) of people and performance.

12. Generally assume the role of a coach rather than waiting to be asked.

13. Help leaders help themselves and provide stretch assignments that go beyond the leader's perceived capacity. Challenging potential leaders is a major value of leadership coaches. It also helps them achieve their goals at a faster and more efficient pace.

Leadership development is a commitment to self-development. It is achieved through lifelong learning, commitment, thinking, and ethical living. Leadership development should be treated as the organization's number one priority. As the leader learns to do by doing, he or she also learns to accept coaching by becoming the coach of others. In coaching we retain the value of reciprocal (mutual, give-and-take, shared, collective) power. It propels the organization into the future by developing new knowledge, new practices, and new thinking about the challenges of the day. Leadership development is an engine for positive change!

Leadership Coaching Characteristics of Someone Else	**Leadership Coaching Characteristics Followers Would See in Me**
1.	1.
2.	2.
3.	3.
4.	4.
5.	5.

Activity 41: Leadership Qualities

Directions: In the following spaces list the qualities of leadership you discovered while studying this section and then discuss these within small groups and with the entire class. With the class, create a master list of these qualities.

QUALITIES YOU DISCOVERED	MASTER LIST

Activity 42: Roadmap

Directions: Review the strategies and methods in this book, especially the conclusions you have reached by completing the activities. Review your vision statement and statement of purpose. When you have completed a thorough review, create a *roadmap* for change by outlining the steps you must take to move from where you are now, to where your vision statement is pulling you. Use the following sequential graphic for this activity:

1. _____

_____

_____

2. _____

_____

_____

3. _____

_____

_____

4. _____

_____

_____

5. _____

_____

_____

6. _____

_____

_____

7. _____

_____

_____

SUMMARY

Leaders Who Grow Leaders . . .

- Believe people can change,

- See us for what we can become, not for what we have been,

- Approach us in terms of the present and future rather than just the past,

- Want us in the game with them, and

- Bring us along one step at a time.

THINGS TO REMEMBER

- A pull style of leadership is costly in terms of time, vulnerability, and exposure, but the rewards are worth it.

- The cure for selfishness is servanthood.

- Real and lasting productivity improvements come from the hearts and minds of people.

- Only that which I give away can I retain as my own.

- The way you get faith from someone is to show faith in that person.

- Cooperation and competition work at cross-purposes.

- You can only have faith in someone to the degree you know them.

- Everyone serves someone or something—the question is who or what?

- There are times when nothing a person can say is nearly so powerful as saying nothing.

- Great leaders don't divest of themselves and invest in others to develop a few good followers; rather, they divest and invest to create a successful generation of leaders.

Bibliography

Allen, James. *As a Man Thinketh.* Sunbooks.com/new/James.htm, 2002.

Annison, Michael H. *Managing the Whirlwind.* Englewood, CO: Medical Group Management Association, 1993.

Antoninums, Marcus Aurelius. *Meditations.*167 A.C.E., translated by George Long. http://classics.mit.edu/Antoninus/meditations.html.

Barnard, Chester I., and K. R. Andrews. *The Functions of the Executive.* Cambridge: Harvard University Press, 1968.

Barton, Bruce. *The Man Nobody Knows.* London: Butler and Tanner, 1925.

Belasco, James. *Teaching the Elephant to Dance: Empowering Change in Your Organization.* New York: Plume, 1991.

Bennis, Warren. *Healthcare Forum Journal* (no date).

———. "Leadership in the 21st Century." *Training,* May 1990.

———. *On Becoming a Leader.* New York: Addison and Wesley, 1989.

———. "Replacing Pornography with Leadership Virtue." "COPs and ACEs." *Executive Excellence.* January 1992.

———. *Teaching Old Dogs New Tricks.* Provo, UT: Executive Excellence, 1999.

———. *Why Leaders Can't Lead.* San Francisco: Jossey-Bass, 1989.

Bennis, Warren, and Burt Narvus. *Leaders: The Strategies for Taking Charge.* New York: Harper & Row, 1985.

Bennis, Warren, and Joan Goldsmith. *Learning to Lead.* New York: Addison and Wesley, 1994.

Bennis, Warren, and Robert Townsend. *Reinventing Leadership.* New York: William Morrow Co., 1995.

Benny, Leonard L. *Discovering the Soul of Service.* New York: The Free Press, 1999.

Blanchard, Kenneth, and Michael O'Connor. *Managing by Values.* New York: William Morrow Co., 1997.

Blanchard, Kenneth, and Norman Vincent Peale. *The Power of Ethical Management.* New York: William Morrow Co., 1988.

Block, Peter. *The Empowered Manager.* San Francisco: Jossey-Bass, 1987.

Brown, Steven W. *13 Fatal Errors Managers Make and How You Can Avoid Them.* Old Tappan, NJ: Fleming H. Revell, 1985.

Burns, James MacGregor. *Leadership.* New York: Harper & Row, 1978.

Campolo, Tony. *Everything You've Heard Is Wrong.* Waco, TX: Word Publishing, 1992.

Capra, Fritjof. *Hidden Connections,* New York: Doubleday, 2000.

Cashman, Kevin. *Leadership from the Inside Out.* Provo, UT: Executive Excellence Publishers, 1998.

Catlette, Bill, and Richard Hadden. *Contented Cows Give Better Milk.*1998.

The Center for Life Cycle Sciences. "Why Vision?" Vol. 4, 1990; "Visionary Leadership," Vol. 5, 1990; "Creating Inspired and Inspiring Vision," Vol. 6, 1990; "Vision Implementation Strategy," Vol. 7,1990.

"Change: The New Metaphysics." *Executive Excellence,* November 1990.

Cherney, Marcia B., and Susan A Tynan, with Ruth Duskin Feldman. *Communicoding.* New York: Donald I. Fine, 1989.

Covey, Stephen R. *The Seven Habits of Highly Effective People.* New York: Simon and Schuster, 1989.

"Creative Leadership." *Executive Excellence,* August 1991.

Deal, Terrence E., and Allan A. Kennedy. *Corporate Cultures: The Rites and Rituals of Corporate Life.* New York: Addison and Wesley, 1982.

"Dealing with the Way Things Are." *Executive Excellence*, (reprint, no date or number).

DePree, Max. *Leadership Is an Art*. New York: Doubleday, 1989.

————. *Leadership Jazz*. New York: Doubleday, 1992.

Drucker, Peter F. *The Effective Executive*. New York: Harper and Row, 1966.

————. *Innovation and Entrepreneurship*. New York: Harper and Row, 1985.

————. *The New Realities*. New York: Harper and Row, 1989.

Eckhart, Meister. See Meister Eckhart Home Page: http://web.wwisp. com/~srshanks/ Meister _Eckhart/

Emerson, Ralph Waldo. Quoted from Cornel West, *The American Evasion of Philosophy: A Genealogy of Pragmatism,* Madison: The University of Wisconsin Press, 1989.

Engstrom, Ted W., and Edward R. Dayton. *The Christian Executive*. Waco, TX: Word Book Publisher, 1979.

Engstrom, Ted W., with Robert C. Larson. *Integrity*. Waco, TX: Word Book Publishers, 1987.

Flower, Joe. "The Chasm between Management and Leadership, A Conversation with Warren Bennis." *Healthcare Forum Journal* (reprint, no date or number).

Ford, Leighton. *Transforming Leadership*. Downers Grove, IL: Intervarsity Press, 1991.

Frankel, Victor. *Man's Search for Meaning*. New York: Beacon Press, 1946.

Freud, Sigmund. *Archives:* http://users.rcn.com/brill/freudarc.html.

Gabor, Andrea. "Interview." *Deming's Quality Manifesto Best of Business Quarterly*, winter 1990/1991.

Galbraith, John Kenneth. Quoted in Annison, Michael H. *Managing the Whirlwind.* Englewood, CO: Medical Group Management Association, 1993.

Gardner, John. *On Leadership*. New York: The Free Press, 1990.

George, Bill. *Authentic Leadership: Rediscovering the Secrets to Creating Lasting Value*. New York: John Wiley & Sons, 2003.

Glass, Bill, and James E. McEachern. *Plan to Win*. Waco, Texas: Word Book Publishers, 1984.

Greenleaf, Robert. *Servant as Leader*. New York: Paulist Press, 1997, 1991.

Grove, Andrew S. *Only the Paranoid Survive*. New York: Doubleday, 1996.

Harris, George. "The Post-Capitalist Executive: An Interview with Peter E Drucker." *Harvard Business Review*, May-June 1993.

Heskett, James L. et al. "Putting the Service-Profit Chain to Work." *Harvard Business Review* March-April 1994.

Hester, Joseph P. *Ethical Leadership for School Administrators and Teachers*. Jefferson, NC: McFarland & Company, Inc., Publishers, 2003.

————. *Talking It Over: A Workbook for Character Development*. Lanham, MD: Scarecrow Press, Inc., 2002.

————. *Teaching for Thinking, A Program for School Improvement Through Teaching Critical Thinking across the Curriculum*. Durham, NC: Carolina Academic Press, 1994.

Hickman, Craig R. *Mind of a Manager—Soul of a Leader*. New York: John Wiley and Sons, Inc. 1990.

Huckabee, Mike, with John Perry. *Character Is the Issue*. Nashville: Broadman and Holman, 1997.

Jung, C. G. *The Basic Writings of C. G. Jung*. New York: Modern Library, 1993.

Juran, J. M. *Juran on Leadership*. New York: The Free Press, 1989.

Kanter, Rosabeth Moss. *When Giants Learn to Dance*. New York: Simon and Schuster, 1989.

Kazuma, Tateisi. *The Eternal Venture Spirit*. Cambridge: Productivity Press, 1989.

Kotter, John. R. *A Force of Change*. New York: The Free Press, 1990.

————. *The Leadership Factor*. New York: The Free Press, 1988.

Kouzes, James M., and Barry Z. Posner. *The Leadership Challenge*. San Francisco: Jossey-Bass, 1987.

Laing, R. D. Quoted in Annison, Michael H. *Managing the Whirlwind.* Englewood, CO: Medical

Group Management Association, 1993.

Leinberger, Paul, and Bruce Tucker. *The New Individualists.* New York: HarperCollins, 1991.

Maccoby, Michael. *The Leader: A New Face for American Management.* New York: Ballantine Publishing, 1983.

Machiavelli, Niccolo. *The Prince.* New York: The Macmillan Company, 1916.

Maxwell, John C. *The 21 Irrefutable Laws of Leadership.* Nashville: Thomas Nelson, 1998.

McCormack, Mark H. *What They Still Don't Teach You at Harvard Business School.* New York: Bantam, 1989.

McCullough, Michael E. "Research on Other-Regarding Virtues, 1998-2002," in Stephen G. Post, et al., editors. *Research on Altruism and Love.* Philadelphia: Templeton Foundation Press, 2003.

Miller, Calvin. *Leadership.* Colorado Springs: NAV Press, 1987.

Miller, Lawrence M. *Barbarians to Bureaucrats.* New York: Clarkson N. Potter, 1989.

Moore, Geoffrey A. *Crossing the Chasm.* New York: Harper Business, 1991.

Naisbitt, John, and Patricia Aburdene. *Re-Inventing the Corporation.* New York: Warner Books, 1985.

Nanus, Burt. *The Leader's Edge: The Seven Keys to Leadership in a Turbulent World.* Chicago: Contemporary Books, 1989.

Pascarella, Perry, and Mark A. Frohman. *The Purpose-Driven Organization.* San Francisco: Jossey-Bass,1989.

Peters, Tom. *Thriving on Chaos.* New York: Knopf, 1987.

Peters, Tom, and Robert H. Wateman, Jr. *In Search of Excellence.* New York: Harper and Row, 1982.

Phillips, Donald T. *Founding Fathers on Leadership.* New York: Warner Books, 1997.

———. *Lincoln on Leadership.* New York: Warner Books, 1992.

Reighard, Dwight. *Discovering Your North Star.* New York: Quantum Leap Publishers, 1998.

Rush, Myron. *Management: A Biblical Approach.* Wheaton, IL: Victor Books, 1983.

———. *Managing to Be the Best.* Wheaton, IL: Victor Books, 1989.

Samples, Bob. *The Metaphoric Mind.* Reading, MA: Addison-Wesley Publishing Company, 1976.

Schaar, John H. *Legitimacy and the Modern State.* New Brunswick, NJ: Transaction Books, 1981.

Schlechty, Philip C. *Schools for the 21st Century: Leadership Imperatives for Educational Reform.* San Francisco: Jossey-Bass, 1990.

Schweitzer, Albert. *Reverence for Life.* New York: Philosophical Library, 1965.

Senge, Peter. "The Leader's New Work: Building Learning Organizations." *Sloan Management Review*, Vol. 32, Number 1, fall 1990.

Sohar, Danah, and Ian Marshall. *The Quantum Society.* New York: William Morrow, 1994.

Solzhenitsyn, Alexander. *One Day in the Life of Ivan Denisovich.* New York: Mass Market Paperback, 1962.

Stanley, Andrew. *Like a Rock: Becoming a Person of Character.* New York: Thomas Nelson, 1997.

———. *The Next Generation Leader.* Sisters, OR: Multnomah, 2003.

Stein, Gertrude. *Lectures in America.* New York: Random House, 1935.

Thomas, Lewis. *The Lives of a Cell.* New York: Bantam Books, 1984.

Toffler, Alvin, and Heidi Toffler. "Supercivilization and Its Discontents," in *Civilization*, F/M 2000.

Towsend, Robert. *Further up the Organization.* New York: Knopf, 1984.

Tribble, Mary (columnist, Business Section). *The Charlotte Observer*, Tuesday, January 4, 2000.

Waitley, Denis E. *Being the Best.* Nashville: Oliver Nelson, 1987.

Waitley, Denis E., and Robert B. Tucker. *Winning the Innovation Game.* Berkeley: Berkeley

Publishing Group, (out of print).

Weatley, Margaret J. *Leadership and the New Science*. San Francisco: Berrett-Koehleer
Publishers, 1994.

Wessel, Peter. *In Place of Absence*. Baltimore: New Poets Series, Chestnut Hills Press, 1990.

Zaleznik, Abraham. *The Managerial Mystique*. New York: Harper and Row, 1989.

About the Authors

H. Darrell Young

After being named president of a public healthcare information systems company (HBO & Company) in the mid-1980s, H. Darrell Young's attention was drawn to the study of leadership. Because of his diverse business background, which includes sales, operations, research, and development, coupled with the onslaught of interconnected, accelerated forces of change, he became acutely aware of the requirement for the development of learning environments that allow for personal development and reinvention. The reinvention tool became leadership and his passion for this tool resulted in *Leadership under Construction*.

In addition, Mr. Young founded and took public a healthcare information company, participated in the development of the University of Georgia's Terry College Leadership Institute, and assisted in the development of a youth leadership program at the University of Georgia Fanning Leadership Institute. He is also cofounder of the Leadership Academy for Cobb County High Schools. His current interest includes helping people help themselves to become leaders by serving as a business advisor, board member, leadership instructor, and certification specialist in leadership development.

Joseph P. Hester

Joseph P. Hester earned a Ph.D. from the University of Georgia in 1973. His career spans public school, college teaching, and public school administration. He is the author of numerous professional articles and over 30 books in education, religion, philosophy, and leadership development. Dr. Hester is a retired educator living in North Carolina and now devotes much of his time to professional writing and training. Hester is the author of *Talking It Over: A Workbook for Character Education,* published by Scarecrow Press in 2002. His latest book is *Ethical Leadership for Public School Administrators and Teachers.* In 2003, he also published *Public School Safety: A Resource Book* and *The Ten Commandments: Legal and Social Issues.*

Workshops are available by contacting Transformance Concepts:
Telephone: (770) 619-1532
Email: *hdyoung@earthlink.net* or *probin@charter.net*
Fax: (770) 730-0822